"Kierkegaard's reputation as a profound religious, poetic, philosophical and psychological thinker and writer is widely recognized, especially in the academic world, but his devastating critique of Christendom is often lost at the level of the institutional church, for which it was primarily intended and where it was and is most needed. Mark Tietjen's book will go a long way toward redressing that lacuna by introducing Kierkegaard specifically as a Christian missionary to contemporary Christians. In it he not only seeks to allay suspicions, fears and misconceptions about Kierkegaard as a philosopher and Christian thinker but also to explicate the basic elements of his thought in a manner that makes it accessible to fellow believers who want to better understand what it means to be a Christian and to deepen their faith in Christ."

Sylvia Walsh, Stetson University

"I often meet young adults who call themselves 'recovering evangelicals,' or, similarly, who explain as quickly as they can up front that they have moved beyond their days in a nondenominational parachurch group. One such student gave me a refrigerator magnet that says: 'Yeah, like Jesus would live in a gated community and attend a mega-church.' Reading Kierkegaard with young Christians caught between the twinned perspectives of idealism and cynicism amplifies Kierkegaard's pastoral voice. Mark Tietjen's book describes, in the vernacular, how Kierkegaard quickens readers to receive the daily gift of a faith that has often been taught either as a cosmic culture battle or as a guide to good manners. This book is an inviting, loving introduction to the writings of a Christian intent on revivifying the faith of the faithful."

Amy Laura Hall, Duke University

"Kierkegaard famously described his task as 'reintroducing Christianity into Christendom.' In this wonderfully rich and clearly written book Mark Tietjen helps us understand what Kierkegaard meant by this, and thereby helps us see how vital it is for the contemporary church to encounter Kierkegaard's thought. Kierkegaard's message will pull us away from complacency and help us understand anew what it means to be a follower of Jesus. Kierkegaard shows us that this is a task for a lifetime; we never 'arrive' short of death, but we can go ever deeper in faith, hope and love."

C. Stephen Evans, Baylor University

"Kierkegaard dismally feared that his writings, which he carefully crafted to affect the individual reader's self-understanding and reorient the reader's heart to Jesus Christ, would fall into the hands of 'the professors' and be turned into some kind of philosophical 'position' that could be debated in seminar rooms and lecture halls to distract its practitioners from attending to the spiritual condition of their souls. 'The professors' have amply fulfilled Kierkegaard's fear, but occasionally a book appears that reflects his original intention for his writings and even helps them to have the intended effect. Tietjen's wise and winsome book is one of them."

Robert C. Roberts, University of Birmingham, UK

"Although the works of Kierkegaard are widely studied by scholars in the academy, Kierkegaard himself was much more interested in speaking to 'ordinary' people, whose company he certainly preferred to that of professors who specialized in obscuring the true nature of Jesus' call to discipleship. With this book, Mark Tietjen succeeds in making Kierkegaard accessible to the people whom Kierkegaard cared about most, those who have an interest in Christianity precisely because they really do want to know what being a follower of Christ entails. Tietjen's work is an excellent guide to one of the most challenging and most profound thinkers of the Christian tradition."

Murray Rae, University of Otago

"I've long believed that Kierkegaard's greatest relevance today is as a kind of prophet—in the sense of a critical, incisive voice—for western Christianity. Mark Tietjen creatively presents the prophetic Kierkegaard as a 'Christian missionary to Christians,' many of whom are deeply suspicious of Kierkegaard. Mark's book is a great resource for Christians, especially those who have been mislead by faulty interpretations of the great thinker. He eloquently shows that Kierkegaard is not just a 'Socratic gadfly,' but also a gadfly for the gospel."

Kyle Roberts, United Theological Seminary of the Twin Cities

"This is the best kind of introduction to Kierkegaard because it shares his goal, that of making us more faithful Christians. Kierkegaard's unique method of doing this was to 'deceive' us into the truth. By giving us sound Christian wisdom for the life of faith that just happens to be Kierkegaardian in word and spirit, Mark Tietjen deceives us into Kierkegaard."

Jack Mulder Jr., Hope College

Kierkegaard

A Christian Missionary to Christians

Mark A. Tietjen

Foreword by Merold Westphal

IVP Academic

An imprint of InterVarsity Press
Downers Grove, Illinois

InterVarsity Press
P.O. Box 1400, Downers Grove, IL 60515-1426
ivpress.com
email@ivpress.com

InterVarsity Press® is the book-publishing division of InterVarsity Christian Fellowship/USA®, a movement of students and faculty active on campus at hundreds of universities, colleges and schools of nursing in the United States of America, and a member movement of the International Fellowship of Evangelical Students. For information about local and regional activities, visit intervarsity.org.

Scripture quotations, unless otherwise noted, are from the New Revised Standard Version of the Bible, copyright 1989 by the Division of Christian Education of the National Council of the Churches of Christ in the USA. Used by permission. All rights reserved.

While any stories in this book are true, some names and identifying information may have been changed to protect the privacy of individuals.

Portions of chapter three were published in Mark A. Tietjen and C. Stephen Evans, "Kierkegaard as a Christian Psychologist," Journal of Psychology and Christianity 30, no. 4 (2011): 274-83. Those portions have been either adapted or reprinted by permission.

Cover design: Cindy Kiple
Interior design: Beth McGill
Images: © Corbis

ISBN 978-0-8308-4097-7 (print)
ISBN 978-0-8308-9951-7 (digital)

Printed in the United States of America ∞

 As a member of the Green Press Initiative, InterVarsity Press is committed to protecting the environment and to the responsible use of natural resources. To learn more, visit greenpressinitiative.org.

Library of Congress Cataloging-in-Publication Data

Names: Tietjen, Mark A., author.
Title: Kierkegaard : a Christian missionary to Christians / Mark A. Tietjen ;
  foreword by Merold Westphal.
Description: Downers Grove : InterVarsity Press, 2016. | Includes index.
Identifiers: LCCN 2015050886 (print) | LCCN 2016001402 (ebook) | ISBN
  9780830840977 (pbk. : alk. paper) | ISBN 9780830899517 (eBook)
Subjects: LCSH: Kierkegaard, Søren, 1813-1855.
Classification: LCC BX4827.K5 T57 2016 (print) | LCC BX4827.K5 (ebook) | DDC
  230/.044092—dc23
LC record available at http://lccn.loc.gov/2015050886

P	23	22	21	20	19	18	17	16	15	14	13	12	11	10	9	8	7	6	5	4	3	2	1
Y	35	34	33	32	31	30	29	28	27	26	25	24	23	22	21	20	19	18	17	16			

To Amy

CONTENTS

FOREWORD

Merold Westphal

Distinguished Professor of Philosophy Emeritus
Fordham University

THIS IS NOT MARK TIETJEN'S FIRST BOOK ON KIERKEGAARD.
In an earlier volume he offered an interpretation of Kierkegaard's writings
that directly challenged a type of reading that in recent years has become
very popular among some academics. It can be called "deconstructive."
The basic idea is that partly because of the very nature of language and
partly because of Kierkegaard's literary style and tactics, his writings
make no substantive claim on our belief and behavior; they rather "teach"
us that every teaching undermines itself in ambiguity and undecidability.
Mark made a compelling critique of such readings. It was an important
contribution to Kierkegaard scholarship, appropriately published by a
university press.[1]

The present volume has a different purpose and is addressed to a different audience: those who are not academics, or at least not philosophers, or at least not Kierkegaard scholars. The intended audience is
Christians who might benefit from hearing Kierkegaard presented as a
missionary to Christians even if they be nonacademics, academics who
are not philosophers or philosophers who are not Kierkegaard scholars.[2]

---

[1]*Kierkegaard, Communication, and Virtue: Authorship as Edification* (Bloomington: Indiana University Press, 2013).

[2]This does not mean that Kierkegaard scholars, such as myself, will not be able to enjoy and learn
from this book.

Kierkegaard's writings conclude with a series of polemical pamphlets that have come to be known as his "attack upon Christendom," though I find this critique present from his earliest publications on. His complaint is not that the churches are not sufficiently orthodox but that they make being a Christian too easy, virtually automatic (if one happens not to be a Jew). They have, in his view, cheapened grace.[3] So, with a wicked twinkle in his eye, he famously says that while everyone else is trying to make it easier to become a Christian, he will devote himself to making it harder. I will return to this theme.

Kierkegaard's writings are very diverse in style, subject matter and purpose. I like to think of them as like the stanzas of a hymn such as, say, "Rock of Ages." Each has its own task, making a different point or a similar point in a different way. But together they make a richly diverse yet coherent whole.[4] Or, to use a different metaphor, each text is like one facet of a beautiful diamond whose oneness is enhanced and not compromised by its manyness. Kierkegaard insisted that serious interpretations of his work take the whole of his authorship into account. Happily, Mark roams gracefully and perceptively throughout the extensive corpus.

There is another plurality in Kierkegaard's authorship that calls for a different metaphor. Mark tells us, importantly, that Kierkegaard is a philosopher, a theologian, a psychologist, a prophet and a poet. But these are not sequential, like stanzas, or spatially separate, like facets; they are simultaneous. A chocolate cake is a better image here. You don't first eat the flour and then the chocolate. You don't have eggs here and butter there. They are mixed together so that with every bite you eat flour and chocolate and butter and eggs and who knows what else.

Kierkegaard tells us, in retrospect, that he is a religious author, more specifically a Christian author. He insists "that I am and was a religious author, that my whole authorship pertains to Christianity, to the issue: becoming a Christian, with direct and indirect polemical aim at that enormous illusion, Christendom" (PV 23; cf. 8, 12). So he is a theologian.

---

[3]There is an important affinity between Kierkegaard and Bonhoeffer's analysis of "cheap grace" in *The Cost of Discipleship.*
[4]Kierkegaard insisted that we interpret each text in the context of his whole authorship. Unlike those gurus who pontificate about Kierkegaard without bothering to read him, Mark has a deep knowledge of that corpus and ranges throughout it effortlessly.

At the same time he is a philosopher, and that in two senses. He engages the thought of important philosophers, especially Hegel and Plato,[5] and he insists on careful conceptual analysis so that, for example, we do not conflate commanded neighbor love with spontaneous and preferential loves such as erotic love and friendship.

At the same time he is a psychologist in the sense of exploring what it means to be a self and how selfhood is not a fait accompli, "an accomplished, presumably irreversible deed or fact,"[6] but rather a task that we may or may not undertake and that we may do well or poorly. Since Kierkegaard is a theologian at the same time as he is a psychologist, he explores what it means to be a self before God[7] and why we should speak of becoming a Christian rather than of being one.[8]

At the same time he is a poet. For him one of the most important aesthetic values is "the interesting." Through such literary devices as narrative, parable, satire, irony and pseudonymity, he sneaks up on the reader with substantial theological, philosophical and psychological claims. Just as with the help of the dialogue form Plato is more fun to read (and easier) than Aristotle, so Kierkegaard is more fun to read (and easier) than his nemesis, Hegel.

At the same time, finally, he is a prophet—in the biblical sense of the term—a social critic who exposes the discrepancy between the moral and religious values a people profess and their daily practice. Early prophets did indeed foretell the loss of national independence that would occur if the people did not change their ways; but their "predictions" were not those of a psychic satisfying curiosity about the future. They were dire warnings of the drastic consequences of continuing in idolatry and the oppression of the poor.

For this dimension of his work, Kierkegaard took Socrates, the gadfly (stinging pest), as his model. He conversed with "the best and the brightest"

---

[5]He sometimes conflates Plato and Socrates while at other times he distinguishes them, making Socrates a hero and a role model.

[6]This definition from *The American Heritage Dictionary of the English Language*.

[7]For a sustained focus on this theme, see Simon D. Podmore, *Kierkegaard and the Self Before God: Anatomy of the Abyss* (Bloomington: Indiana University Press, 2011).

[8]The analogy with twelve-step programs that teach followers to say "I am a recovering alcoholic" is apt here.

of Athens, who were complacently content that their practices were grounded in a solid knowledge of the truth. Through his sharp (not especially gentlemanly) questions, Socrates showed that they didn't know what they were talking about. Perhaps Kierkegaard does not explicitly take the biblical prophets as his model because, while they were able to say, "Thus says the Lord," he insisted that he spoke "without authority."

This brings us back to Kierkegaard's announced goal of making it harder rather than easier, all but automatic, to become a Christian. It is precisely by the thorough intermixing of his theological, philosophical, psychological, literary and prophetic roles that he seeks to do this. We might say that his literary ingenuity and his prophetic pugnacity are the leaven that leavens the loaf of his theological, philosophical and psychological claims. The former makes them interesting, but it is the latter that gives them their bite. It is in his role as a prophet that he makes it harder to become a Christian.

So how in particular does he do this? Let me count the ways, or at least a few of them.[9] First, he insists that faith is not merely a task but the task of a lifetime. In this life we never graduate from the school of faith. This does not mean that faith is not a gift. Kierkegaard thinks that the whole of life is a gift and a task. The title of his most widely read and discussed book comes from a text with just that point. "Work out [my task] your own salvation with fear and trembling; for it is God who is at work in you [God's gift], enabling you both to will and to work [my task] for his good pleasure" (Phil 2:12-13).[10]

When I was in sixth grade I received a trombone as a birthday gift; but of course that set me to the task of learning to play it, first in private lessons and then in a very good junior high band program. When I got to high school the choir provided a far better musical experience than the band, so I abandoned the trombone and was free of that task. Kierkegaard would say it is just at the point where faith ceases to be an ongoing task

---

[9]In *Kierkegaard's Concept of Faith* (Grand Rapids: Eerdmans, 2014) I have described twelve facets of faith in Kierkegaard's writings, each of which, properly understood, cuts against the grain of a complacent Christendom.

[10]I like "to will and to work" better than "to will and to do" (KJV) or "to will and to act" (NIV) not only for its alliteration but also for the reminder that the doing and acting that good intentions require is work. It takes discipline and effort.

of deeper understanding and more faithful practice that we have in fact abandoned it, no matter how deep our denial.

He has a satire of those who wish to be free from "continual striving," to reach a point where they can live happily ever after—on autopilot.[11] "For most people, life changes when they have come to a certain point in their searching. They marry, they enter occupations, in consequence of which they must out of decency finish something, must have results because shame before people bids them have results. So they believe that they themselves actually have arrived." Like Aesop, he adds the moral of the story. "Only he really has style who is never finished" (CUP 1:85-86).

We learn, sometimes the hard way, that marriage and parenting are tasks of a lifetime, responsibilities that change but do not disappear with the passage of time. Those of us who are privileged to continue practicing our vocations into retirement discover, like veteran athletes and accomplished musicians, that our work does not require less discipline and effort just because we are no longer rookies. Kierkegaard thinks that since the life of faith is life before God (*coram Deo*), it too must be a life of continuing education and exertion.

Second, Kierkegaard insists that this task involves both our beliefs and our behaviors. In *Concluding Unscientific Postscript* he distinguishes Religiousness A from Religiousness B. The former is an existentially serious form of religion in which one is *simultaneously* Absolutely related to what is Absolute and only Relatively related to what is Relative, but without anything distinctively Christian involved in understanding this task. Religiousness B includes Religiousness A but interprets the very abstract notion of the Absolute ("May the Force be with you") in terms of the God-man, Jesus of Nazareth, as fully human and divine, "the only Son of God . . . begotten not made, of one Being with the Father."[12] Like Martin Luther, Kierkegaard emphasizes that this not only goes beyond but also against natural, unaided human reason. It is paradoxical; for pagans,[13] even offensive.

---

[11]I recently learned that "robot pilot" is a synonym for "autopilot."

[12]From the Nicene Creed.

[13]Today we might say secularists. Kierkegaard likes to speak disparagingly of paganism just before he points out the extent to which Christendom has become pagan, or, as we might put it, how secular churches have become.

Of course, for those effectively socialized into Christianity from childhood, this is an easy belief, though liberal Christians may not take the deity of Christ seriously enough and conservative Christians may not take his humanity seriously enough. The rub comes in those writings that present what I like to call Religiousness C.[14] Of course, it includes Religiousness B. Jesus is still God incarnate. But in addition to being the paradox to be believed, he is also the pattern to be imitated. This is where, even for those who have been Christians since they sang "Climb, Climb up Sunshine Mountain" in Sunday School, becoming a Christian becomes the task of a lifetime and by no means an easy one.

Religiousness C is especially prominent in just those texts to which Mark has given special attention: *Works of Love, Practice in Christianity, For Self-Examination* and *Judge for Yourself!* These are excellent places to begin reading Kierkegaard. Although they come later, these works present the religious faith presupposed by such philosophically challenging works as *Fear and Trembling, Philosophical Fragments, Concluding Unscientific Postscript* and *The Sickness unto Death.*

Third, Kierkegaard makes becoming a Christian harder by the way he distinguishes the ethical stage or existence sphere from the religious.[15] He does so in two ways. First, unlike the ethical, the religious takes sin seriously as sin. "As soon as sin emerges, ethics founders precisely on repentance" (FT 98; cf. CA 17).[16] We encounter the absence of sin consciousness in the paganism/secularism of our everyday life. When a politician or an athlete is caught cheating, whether through adultery, bribery, campaign fraud, DUI, performance-enhancing drugs or some other advantage that is against the rules, sexual assault, domestic

---

[14]See my "Kierkegaard's Teleological Suspension of Religiousness B," in *Foundations of Kierkegaard's Vision of Community,* ed. George B. Connell and C. Stephen Evans (Atlantic Highlands, NJ: Humanities Press, 1992), 110-29.

[15]Mark importantly reminds us that the aesthetic, the ethical and the religious are "stages" in the sense of a kind of logical progression. They are not the stages of a developmental psychology, more or less inevitable stages on life's way. We are born aesthetes, in Kierkegaard's sense. A baby's life is good when she has a full tummy and a dry bottom. But as *Either/Or* argues, the ethical is a sphere of existence that we enter only insofar as we choose to, and this is even more true of the religious.

[16]At CA 117, Kierkegaard expands on this by saying that the concept of sin requires repentance and repentance requires atonement, a distinctively religious concept.

violence, even shoplifting, we know what will happen. After strident and indignant denials, sometimes years of lying, the culprit will issue a public statement acknowledging that "I have made some mistakes."[17]

This is what philosophers call a category mistake. It is a mistake to think that eight times seven is fifty-four or that Copenhagen is the capital of Norway. The appropriate language for these kinds of behavior includes terms like cheating, lying, committing crimes, doing wrong, violating the rights of others. These would be, in Kierkegaard's vocabulary, ethical terms, not religious. They are about duty, responsibility, right and wrong in a moral sense that isn't necessarily religious. "I-have-made-some-mistakes" talk doesn't even rise to that level.

A clear religious understanding of sin intensifies the notions of duty, responsibility, right and wrong by placing the self in question before God. In doing so it provides clarity and support for the appropriate ethical language required by the examples given above. It does so precisely by insisting that sin, like cheating, is a matter of the will and not just of the intellect. So, while religion is not reducible to ethics, it provides a (possibly essential) support for ethical self-understanding. Socrates, here no hero to Kierkegaard, espoused the thesis that virtue is knowledge, implying that vice is ignorance. If we know the good, we will do it (SUD 87-96). If we fail to do it, it is because we "made a mistake." Kierkegaard rejects this view and even uses the strong language of defiance to place sin's roots in the will. But insofar as sin against God or cheating in the human sphere is knowingly doing wrong, the language of defiance is just calling a spade a spade. The culture of mistakes makes life too easy. What's needed is not repentance and atonement but the rehabilitation of one's image.

But Kierkegaard also distinguishes the ethical from the religious in another way. In *Fear and Trembling* he speaks of Abraham's faith as a teleological suspension of the ethical. This is simpler than it sounds. It means, quite simply, that ethical norms are authoritative but only relatively; they can be trumped by religious imperatives, since our only absolute duty is to God.

---

[17]Even in the passive voice, as in Nixon's infamous "mistakes were made."

So what is the ethical realm whose imperatives do not, at least not necessarily, come from God? Kierkegaard identifies the ethical with the universal. If we are reading carelessly we will take this to signify some universally valid moral rule, tied to no particular culture, tradition or institutional authority. We often think of human rights or the golden rule in this way. If we've done a little philosophy, we might think of Plato's forms or Kant's categorical imperative. Readers are often puzzled, if not offended, by the notion that the religious can trump the ethical in this sense.

A more careful reading will show that Kierkegaard has something quite different in mind. He goes out of his way to identify the ethical domain under discussion as Hegel's.[18] Hegel thinks that human reason is embedded in particular historical contexts. He defines philosophy as "its own time comprehended in thought."[19] So for him the ethical is the universal, not in the sense of an abstract, ahistorical principle, but as the laws and customs of a particular people. Kierkegaard gives five good examples of what Hegel means by the universal: one's nation, state, society, church or sect. The universal is a human community, secular or religious, to which we belong as individuals. For Hegel the ethical, the norms of such communities, is the highest norm for human life. In distinguishing the ethical (in this sense) from the religious, Kierkegaard is saying that for biblical faith (Abraham here) no human community, even one's religious community, has such absolute authority. Only God has.

How does this make it harder to become a Christian? It means that no human community, secular or religious, is a completely reliable guide to how we should live our lives. The moral support, what sociologists call a plausibility structure, we get from living in the midst of like-minded people, may be mistaken, even demonic. As with the prophets of old, the voice of God may place the gospel in opposition to business as usual in our nation, state, society, church or sect. Christianity is inherently counter cultural, since every human community is doubly relative in its authority:

---

[18]Kierkegaard speaks differently about the ethical in other texts. His own ethical teaching is best found in *Works of Love* and is an essential part of the religious life.
[19]*Philosophy of Right*, preface.

like the individuals who make it up, it is finite and it is fallen. We are deprived of the comfort and complacency we might otherwise derive from belonging to a "Christian" nation and an orthodox church.

Fourth and finally, Kierkegaard makes it harder to be a preacher. For a long time I've said that someone should do a doctoral dissertation on Kierkegaard's critique of the clergy; so I'm pleased that Mark has specifically addressed this issue. It is sometimes said that the pastoral task is to comfort the afflicted and to afflict the comfortable. Every pastor knows how much easier it is to do the first than to do the second.

In his farewell to the Ephesian elders, Paul says, "For I have not hesitated to proclaim to you the whole will of God" (Acts 20:27 NIV). This includes the parts we are least eager to hear. The faithful preacher will, in the tradition of Amos and Isaiah, Jesus and Paul, find it necessary, if not easy, to challenge the social and ecclesial complacencies of his or her congregation. After all, when Jesus came preaching the good news, the first word was the bad news: "Repent" (Mk 1:15).

As it turns out, this difficulty does not pertain only to the clergy. Congregations can make it clear whether or not they are willing to have their pastor afflict the comfortable as well as comfort the afflicted.

In the end Kierkegaard is a good Lutheran. If making it harder to become a Christian is his interpretation of the law, he knows that the purpose of the law is to lead us to the gospel. Among his most beautiful reflections on the gospel are his communion meditations. So for devotional reading I highly recommend his *Discourses at the Communion on Fridays*, translated by Sylvia Walsh (Bloomington: Indiana University Press, 2011).

ABBREVIATIONS

BA   *The Book on Adler.* Edited and translated by Howard V. Hong and Edna H. Hong. Princeton, NJ: Princeton University Press, 1998.

CA   *The Concept of Anxiety.* Edited and translated by Reidar Thomte. Princeton, NJ: Princeton University Press, 1980.

CD   *Christian Discourses* and *The Crisis and a Crisis in the Life of an Actress.* Edited and translated by Howard V. Hong and Edna H. Hong. Princeton, NJ: Princeton University Press, 1997.

CUP   *Concluding Unscientific Postscript to Philosophical Fragments.* Edited and translated by Howard V. Hong and Edna H. Hong. Princeton, NJ: Princeton University Press, 1992.

EO   *Either/Or.* Edited and translated by Howard V. Hong and Edna H. Hong. 2 vols. Princeton, NJ: Princeton University Press, 1987.

FSE   *For Self-Examination; Judge for Yourself!* Edited and translated by Howard V. Hong and Edna H. Hong. Princeton, NJ: Princeton University Press, 1990.

FT   *Fear and Trembling.* Edited by C. Stephen Evans and Sylvia Walsh. Translated by Sylvia Walsh. Cambridge: Cambridge University Press, 2006.

JFY   *Judge for Yourself!* See *For Self-Examination.*

JP   *Søren Kierkegaard's Journals and Papers.* Edited and translated by Howard V. Hong and Edna H. Hong. 7 vols. Bloomington: Indiana University Press, 1967–1978.

PC   *Practice in Christianity.* Edited and translated by Howard V. Hong and Edna H. Hong. Princeton, NJ: Princeton University Press, 1991.

PF   *Philosophical Fragments.* Edited and translated by Howard V. Hong and Edna H. Hong. Princeton, NJ: Princeton University Press, 1985.

PV   *The Point of View for My Work as an Author*, "The Single Indi-
        vidual," *On My Work as an Author* and *Armed Neutrality*.
        Edited and translated by Howard V. Hong and Edna H. Hong.
        Princeton, NJ: Princeton University Press, 1998.

SUD   *The Sickness unto Death*. Edited and translated by Howard V.
        Hong and Edna H. Hong. Princeton, NJ: Princeton University
        Press, 1980.

UDVS   *Upbuilding Discourses in Various Spirits*. Edited and translated
        by Howard V. Hong and Edna H. Hong. Princeton, NJ:
        Princeton University Press, 1993.

WL   *Works of Love*. Edited and translated by Howard V. Hong and
        Edna H. Hong. Princeton, NJ: Princeton University Press, 1995.

INTRODUCTION

A PERSONAL STORY

For a short time during my studies in college I considered the idea of becoming a Bible translator. I had recently taken courses in biblical Greek and enjoyed it immensely, and the idea of spending extended amounts of time working further in the language was an exciting prospect. I attended Palm Beach Atlantic University (then College), which boasts one of the most service-oriented student bodies in the country. At the time every student was required to perform forty-five hours of community service each year of college. Given the Christian roots of the school, many students chose to go on mission trips all over the country and world. Between my consideration of being a Bible translator and a college setting where students were deeply invested in mission work, I spent a lot of time thinking about the idea of missions and the commission Jesus issues in the Gospel of Matthew. On the one hand I felt this was mandatory work for the Christian—after all, Jesus doesn't *suggest* people "go and make disciples of all nations"—he doesn't say, "I have a nice idea . . . how about doing this." Rather, he commands it.

But I also had growing reservations about mission work, about how it was often carried out. On a study abroad trip to Russia my junior year, I recall running into some Christian missionaries in St. Petersburg who seemed to be spreading the gospel of American culture more than anything. These were people who, because they could easily afford it, hired personal drivers to take them around town rather than, like us students, use public transportation, where they would come nose to nose with people. There was a cultural loftiness that seemed to infect whatever message they had come to tell, and I remember thinking to myself, if I were a Russian I wouldn't listen to them.

It was in the midst of this tension between recognizing the Christian's obligation to mission work, and yet the deep problems that accompany this sort of activity, when I came across a quotation in *Campus Life* magazine that resonated deep within me: "Unless the individual is changed and steadily continues to change in himself, his introduction of Christianity into a country is no more a religious act than any ordinary act of conquest." What I appreciated about this quote was that it implied that mission work must at all times be self-directed just as much, if not more, than at the "target" audience. It implied that one does not speak to others about religious matters from a position of superiority and expect to succeed—either in winning a convert or in pleasing God. It suggested to me that perhaps the best way to spread the faith is to preach a little less and love a lot more, to demonstrate one's commitment to God and his kingdom through acts of thoughtful Christian service.

A few years later I followed my love of biblical Greek to Princeton Theological Seminary, with an interest, now, in becoming a New Testament scholar. For various reasons, this interest was—like the translator idea—short-lived. While at seminary, however, someone recommended I take a course that was different from most other courses at the time—it was a seminar on the Danish philosopher Søren Kierkegaard. The only reason I took the course was because I had no idea what I was doing at seminary, and as it turns out, in this course I got an idea. Dr. James Loder, a wonderful teacher and mentor whose faith was unusually transparent, taught the seminar. In our exploration of Kierkegaard's writings I was impressed with a number of things—his penetration of the human condition, his honesty about the difficulty of being honest with oneself, his willingness to ask challenging questions while remaining faithful, his reminder that the Christian belief in the incarnation is wild and radical, and the priority of loving one's neighbor over the nailing down of theological minutia. All of these things and more pushed me in the direction of studying Kierkegaard further, and ultimately toward the formal study of philosophy.

Not too long after I took the course with Dr. Loder, I was rummaging through a box of junk from college, and in that box I found a scrap of paper, a page cut out from a magazine, with silly-putty stains on the corners from where it had been affixed to my dorm-room door. On the paper was the quotation from *Campus Life* I had encountered during college. At the bottom was the source, a source I had either overlooked or forgotten and certainly couldn't pronounce. Of course the quote was from Kierkegaard.[1]

PURPOSE AND PLAN

In the two decades since I first came across that quotation I have become convinced that Kierkegaard not only has something to say to me but to all who call themselves Christians. In Job 8, one of Job's much-maligned friends, Bildad, offers a nugget of wisdom that still rings true more than three millennia later:

> For inquire, please, of bygone ages,
>   and consider what the fathers have searched out.
> For we are but of yesterday and know nothing,
>   for our days on earth are a shadow.
> Will they not teach you and tell you
>   and utter words out of their understanding? (Job 8:8-10 ESV)

As the people of God Christians are called to seek wisdom from God's people of earlier times. Whether in the stories of Scripture, the writings of theologians, or the counsel of a parent or grandparent, God speaks to us through those who have journeyed before us. In terms of Christian history Søren Kierkegaard is a relatively recent voice, though I strongly suspect his thought offers a timely challenge and corrective to the pervasive cultural Christianity and endless chatter of Christianese that abounds in much of America.

Bearing in mind that Kierkegaard in particular and philosophy in general can be difficult and intimidating undertakings for the uninitiated, I have written this book not for scholars and professors but for everyday people. Kierkegaard has been accused of being confusing, long-

---

[1]CUP 433.

winded and contradictory, and while I think these accusations are mostly cheap shots, I fully admit that there are any number of other Christian authors that are easier going. Because Kierkegaard participates in long-running conversations in philosophy and theology, his writing makes use of technical concepts and language that will have little meaning to those who do not regularly read such material. For that reason, I have done my best to avoid Kierkegaardian or otherwise philosophical jargon; instead I've aimed to translate his words and concepts into a language Christians today will comprehend without too much difficulty. Though this might earn the ire of the Kierkegaard scholar, I am guessing it will come as welcome news to my reader.

This book is not intended as an introduction to Kierkegaard's thought; it is not at all concerned with the all-too-interesting life of Kierkegaard; and it does not explore Kierkegaard solely as a philosopher. Rather, his thought is presented in such a way that the reader might gain insight into how better to live a Christian life. In chapter one I introduce Kierkegaard, explaining a bit about his life and thought and addressing some concerns Christians may have about studying him. Several Christian writers have offered warnings about interacting with Kierkegaard, claiming his thought is unbiblical or dangerous. I take up a number of those issues directly. Chapters two through five are arranged according to central themes of Kierkegaard's corpus, each of which is central to the life of the Christian. Chapter two concerns theology: Who is Jesus and what mistakes plague our understanding of him, his gift of salvation to us and his work in our life? Chapter three explores Kierkegaard's psychology, including the following sorts of questions: What sort of thing is a human self? How does the self flourish, and how is the self related to God? Chapter four takes up the communication of Christian truth to the world: How might I faithfully testify to God's love and saving grace to the world around me? Chapter five addresses the dominant concept of Kierkegaard's Christian ethics, love.

1

KIERKEGAARD

Friend to Christians?

My goal is to convince Christians as I have been convinced that Søren Kierkegaard is a voice that should be sought and heard for the edification of the church. As a philosopher and a Christian, however, I am familiar with the hesitation some in the church have about entertaining insights from philosophy. *What good is philosophy in the first place, and how can philosophy help one become a better Christian? Isn't philosophy a never-ending quest for truth, and if so, how does that square with the Christian belief that Jesus is the truth, that God is the Alpha and Omega, beginning and end? Doesn't philosophy teach that any opinion is equally valid as any other so long as one gives reasons to support it, no matter what those reasons are?* These are genuine worries worthy of consideration.

On the other hand, some Christians may hold philosophy in a positive light, but they are skeptical that Kierkegaard is a voice that can be trusted. *Isn't he the father of existentialism and thus intellectual kin to atheists like Jean-Paul Sartre and Albert Camus? Or, isn't he a postmodernist, and doesn't postmodernism clash with Christianity?* Some of these more specific concerns about Kierkegaard have been voiced by a handful of influential Christian theologians and pastors over the past half-century. Kierkegaard's writings, for them, would be the last place to turn for guidance and insight into Christian faith. We shall address some of those views as well. First, however, let us begin with a very brief sketch of Kierkegaard's life.

WHO WAS KIERKEGAARD THE PERSON?

Søren Aabye Kierkegaard (SUR-in OH-buh KEER-kuh-goh) was born in Copenhagen, Denmark, May 5, 1813, at the outset of an era of Danish history known as the Golden Age, "a period of literary and artistic splendor, of a cultural blossoming" that would produce the likes of Hans Christian Andersen, the renowned author of children's tales; Nikolai Grundtvig, popular educational and ecclesiastical reformer and prolific hymnodist; and Bertel Thorvaldsen, the neoclassical sculptor.[1] The greatest influence on Kierkegaard's life was his father, Michael Pedersen Kierkegaard (1756–1838), who had seven children in all with Søren's mother, Michael's second wife, Anne Sørensdatter Lund (1768–1834). Michael Kierkegaard was heir to a hosier business and was quite successful with it, and as a result Søren never had to work for his income. Kierkegaard recalls being "favored in every way with regard to mental capacity and outward circumstances" (PV 80). Fifty-six at the time of his youngest son's birth, Michael encouraged Søren in Christian faith in a most rigid and heavy-handed sort of way. Yet, in spite of some questionable excesses, Søren seemed generally grateful for his spiritual upbringing insofar as he received a "decisive impression of the essentially Christian," including especially the idea that God is a God of love (BA 138). Thus does Kierkegaard recount that his relationship with Christianity "was closely linked to my relationship with my father, the person I most deeply loved" (PV 80).

Kierkegaard was reared as a Lutheran and member of the Danish state church, and the family had deep admiration for their pastor, Bishop Jacob Peter Mynster, curate at the Church of Our Lady in Copenhagen. Kierkegaard recalls in his journals how Mynster's sermons were read as devotionals by his family and how his father encouraged him to memorize sermons he heard in church (JP 6:6627, 6355). Michael also took the family to Moravian meetings, "giving the young Søren," C. Stephen Evans writes, "a strong dose of what might loosely be termed 'evangelical pietism' to leaven Lutheran orthodoxy."[2] The

---

[1]Bruce Kirmmse, *Kierkegaard in Golden Age Denmark* (Bloomington: Indiana University Press, 1990), 1.
[2]C. Stephen Evans, *Kierkegaard: An Introduction* (Cambridge: Cambridge University Press, 2009), 4-5.

Kierkegaard family would attend church at the great cathedral Sunday morning and then participate in Moravian meetings Sunday evening, where the latter often involved a "song service" in which no sermons were preached, but where hymns were sung by congregation members from memory.[3] It is reasonable to suppose that the Moravian themes of repentance, the consciousness of sin, joy at forgiveness, witnessing and martyrdom—each of which we find emphasized in Kierkegaard's writings—were deeply impressed on Kierkegaard through these services. Sylvia Walsh summarizes the strong Moravian influence on Kierkegaard's thought: "What seems to have impressed him most . . . was the way they put their beliefs into practice, especially those who were willing to leave everything to preach the gospel in foreign lands and to become martyrs for their cause."[4] Kierkegaard continued to worship in the state church until the year before his death, when his criticisms of official Christianity grew far more harsh.

Given Kierkegaard's rearing, it should come as no surprise that his father wanted Søren to pursue the study of theology, which he did at the University of Copenhagen. Apparently in little hurry, Kierkegaard took ten years to complete his degree, which included attending lectures not only on biblical exegesis, hermeneutics and dogmatic theology, but a number of areas in philosophy, including ancient philosophy, aesthetics and logic.[5] Perhaps part of the delay owed to Kierkegaard's wandering away from faith in the mid-1830s and his struggles with doubt, drunkenness, suicidal thoughts and sexual sin. Though his journals leave an incomplete record of these experiences, the apparent autobiographical nature of many of Kierkegaard's published writings have led scholars to draw all sorts of conclusions about this time period. Among the more persuasive claims is Walter Lowrie's observation that when Kierkegaard portrays immature and lascivious lifestyles with authenticity, consistency and even respect, Kierkegaard is not only drawing on his own past but

---

[3]Andrew J. Burgess, "Kierkegaard, Brorson, and Moravian Music," in *International Kierkegaard Commentary*, vol. 20, *Practice in Christianity* (Macon, GA: Mercer University Press, 2004), 211-43.
[4]Sylvia Walsh, *Kierkegaard: Thinking Christianly in an Existential Mode* (Oxford: Oxford University Press, 2009), 5.
[5]Ibid., 7.

in doing he has "satirized himself."[6] As we shall see in chapter three, one of the virtues of Kierkegaard's reflections on human existence is the honesty with which he explores a variety of different life-views.

By 1838 Kierkegaard's faith seems to have reemerged, and with unusual detail he records in his journal at precisely 10:30 a.m., May 19,

> There is an *indescribable joy* that glows all through us just as inexplicably as the apostle's exclamation breaks forth for no apparent reason: "Rejoice, and again I say, Rejoice."—Not a joy over this or that, but the soul's full outcry "with tongue and mouth and from the bottom of the heart" . . . a joy which cools and refreshes like a breath of air. (JP 6:120 [#5324])

Lowrie notes the report of a pastor that a few weeks following this journal entry, Kierkegaard, having taken considerable time off, returned to church for confession and communion, giving the impression that like so many Christians reared in the church, there is a time of revolt and then a time of contrition and renewed faith. Though one can only speculate as to the cause of the immense joy he describes, from a Christian perspective it is not difficult to imagine that the joy of his salvation has been restored (Ps 51:12), that the weight of sin has been lifted, that he has received anew Christ's gift of forgiveness and new life. On completing his degree, Kierkegaard spent a year in seminary, which would qualify him for ordination. Then immediately afterward he decided to pursue his interests in philosophy further and wrote a dissertation titled *The Concept of Irony with Continual Reference to Socrates*, which earned him the magister's degree, or the equivalent of a PhD.

Besides his father, the second major character in Kierkegaard's life story was Regine Olsen, his onetime fiancée and lifelong inspiration. Nearly the moment Kierkegaard proposed to Regine in 1840, he concluded he had made a grave mistake—that in fact he was not cut out for married life. Although in our day a broken engagement comes with little negative social effect, in nineteenth-century Denmark such an event caused quite a stir. Kierkegaard felt responsible for the trouble he caused Regine, and very clearly he still loved her. Thus, to deflect attention and blame from her, Kierkegaard took on a public persona of bachelor-

---

[6]Walter Lowrie, *A Short Life of Kierkegaard* (Princeton, NJ: Princeton University Press, 1942), 93.

scoundrel about town and appeared to have been rather successful (though apparently he did not fool Regine). Seven years later Regine would marry Frederik Schlegel and then, just months before Kierkegaard's death, in November 1855, the couple would move to the Danish West Indies, where Frederik was appointed governor. On reflection Kierkegaard came to understand the broken engagement as freeing him to put to use his God-given intellectual ability. Given fractured relationships with his father and would-be spouse, Kierkegaard viewed himself and his life's work not unlike those who take vows in a religious order: "This, my God-relationship, is in many ways the happy love of my unhappy and troubled life" (PV 71).[7]

One of the primary causes of trouble in Kierkegaard's life came to be known as the *Corsair* affair. *The Corsair* was a widely circulated satirical paper known for its anonymous commentary on a variety of social and political issues. After one of his books, *Stages on Life's Way* (1845), received a negative review, a provoked Kierkegaard sparred back, going so far as outing the author who had anonymously published the critique. *The Corsair* responded by attacking Kierkegaard below the belt—by printing caricatured cartoons of him (particularly the uneven length of his trousers) and making him out to be a lunatic. Up to this point in time Kierkegaard was well known for walking around the city and engaging in frequent conversation with a variety of everyday people. The *Corsair* event put an end to these constitutionals, as the public joined in on the finger pointing and grinning. Reflecting on the pain of this experience, Kierkegaard writes,

> One must see it close up, the callousness with which otherwise kind people act in the capacity of the public because their participation or non-participation seems to them a trifle—a trifle that with the contributions of the many becomes the monster. One must see how no attack is so feared as that of laughter . . . because more than any other this attack isolates the one attacked. (PV 65)

---

[7]It is beyond the scope of this book and interest of this author to engage in psychological analysis of Kierkegaard's closest relationships, though many others have not resisted this temptation. For a hefty dose of such analysis, see Joakim Garff's *Søren Kierkegaard: A Biography*, trans. Bruce Kirmmse (Princeton, NJ: Princeton University Press, 2007).

Besides giving up his public presence in town, Kierkegaard gave up the dream of becoming a country pastor, a dream that had surfaced over and over again (and would resurface later). Despite the seminary training in his background, the *Corsair* experience seemed to solidify the conviction that he was to continue writing, no matter the public scorn he would endure.

For a few more years following the *Corsair* run-in, Kierkegaard continued to produce an immense amount of work. One of his last major writings, *Practice in Christianity* (1850), would bring to culmination a major theme in his work that has come to be known as his "attack upon Christendom." Kierkegaard came to view the state church as a poor reflection of New Testament Christianity, and his criticism intensified on the occasion of the eulogizing of Mynster as a "witness to the truth." Although Kierkegaard respected Mynster, he fervently believed that being a "witness to the truth" coincided with a life of self-denial and suffering like the lives of the disciples and Christ himself, and yet the established church, much like the church of the Roman emperor Constantine, had the favor of the powerful. In the least Kierkegaard desired for the church of his day to concede that its reflection of New Testament Christianity was faint: such a sign of repentance would indirectly validate that the church's heart was leaning the right direction. But of course neither Mynster nor his successor and eulogizer Hans Lassen Martensen would admit such a thing, especially on the request of an unemployed, self-important son of a hosier with uneven trousers.

Over the last few years of his life Kierkegaard's financial situation grew tight, though he continued to believe that he would never need to work to earn a living. At the age of forty-two, Kierkegaard passed out in the street and died just a few weeks later in the hospital. Keeping up his attack on Christendom until the very end, Kierkegaard famously refused to receive communion on his deathbed from those representing the state church.

Much more could be said about Kierkegaard's life, but I will leave that to the biographers. I conclude this brief sketch by drawing attention to Kierkegaard's vocation as a writer. In his short autobiographical book *On My Work as an Author*, he states, "'Before God,' religiously, when I speak with myself, I call my whole work as an author my own upbringing and development, but not in the sense as if I were now complete or completely finished with regard to needing upbringing and development" (12).

While I have pointed to decisive influences in Kierkegaard's life—his father, his minister, his fiancée—and decisive experiences—his church life, education and spiritual struggles—Kierkegaard's ongoing relationship with God, including particularly his sense of calling not to the pastorate but to a career of writing, must contextualize these other factors. Though much like Paul Kierkegaard concedes he is a woeful sinner, he nevertheless believes God has given him not just rare poetic ability but uncommon insight into the human condition and the spiritual malaise and hypocrisy that plagued the church of his day. In fact, the artistry and the observations commend Kierkegaard to us today, or so I plan to show. If the major figure in Kierkegaard's story is God, as he himself might claim, then why have some Christians viewed him with suspicion? First, though, let us back up one step and ask whether the Christian should worry about philosophy itself.

SHOULD THE CHRISTIAN BE SUSPICIOUS OF PHILOSOPHY?[8]

Perhaps as far back as the time the great pre-Socratic philosopher Thales (624–546 BCE) fell into a well while contemplating the heavens, popular opinion of philosophers and their work has ranged from dismissive to perplexed to suspicious. Once again we might imagine our fictitious objector asking: *How does contemplating the heavens, or working out logical paradoxes, or incessantly asking "but why?," or questioning basic truths everyone knows, contribute to the common good? Why should anyone trust a bunch of navel-gazers who, it seems, do not quite live on earth, who lack everyday common sense and experience? Sure, philosophers seem like smart people, but their smarts don't serve any tangible good. Philosophers hang out in the clouds, ivory towers and, apparently, wells.*

---

[8]Some readers may puzzle over this section; for example, those who have studied in Catholic colleges and universities in the United States or those who have matriculated through European universities, where philosophy plays a more significant role in a general education curriculum. This section is written with the Protestant American reader in mind, who may have been influenced by the many and various anti-intellectual strains in evangelical Christianity over the past several decades. Other readers may wish to proceed to the subsequent section.

Add to these criticisms specifically Christian concerns: *philosophy is a secular activity; surely it is not essential for Christians. And, surely for those Christians who wish to dabble in it, there is great risk. Nothing is sacred to the philosopher, after all.* No one expresses this view of philosophy quite like the Roman theologian Tertullian (circa 160–circa 225 CE), who lived just a few generations after Christ:

> What is there in common between Athens and Jerusalem? Between the Academy and the church? Our system of beliefs comes from the Porch of Solomon, who himself taught that it was necessary to seek God in the simplicity of the heart. . . . We have no need for curiosity after Jesus Christ, nor for inquiry after the gospel. When we believe, we desire to believe nothing further.[9]

If, as the Protestant Reformers would claim more than a millennium later, we are saved by grace *alone*, justified through faith *alone*, able to learn Christian doctrine through Scripture *alone*, and come to God the Father through Christ *alone*, then at best philosophy is superfluous and at worst a potential idol and the path to what, Christianly understood, is ignorance, not truth. If, as King Solomon wrote, fear of the Lord is the beginning of wisdom (Prov 1:7), then what use or benefit could there be from any discipline that does not start with faith?

Tertullian's position, one I would describe as an informed antiphilosophical position (as opposed to an *uninformed*, anti-intellectualist position), was by no means the consensus opinion of the ancient church, and eventually the overwhelming majority of church theologians would come to reject it. In his own day Tertullian's position was contested by Clement of Alexandria (circa 150–circa 215 CE), who viewed secular learning as a means by which God drew a particular pagan culture to himself.

> For God is the source of all good things, some directly (as with the Old and New Testaments), and some indirectly (as with philosophy). But it might be that philosophy was given to the Greeks immediately and directly, until such time as the Lord should also call the Greeks. For

---

[9]Tertullian, in Alister McGrath, ed., *The Christian Theology Reader*, 3rd ed. (Oxford: Blackwell, 2007), 6.

philosophy acted as a "custodian" to bring the Greeks to Christ, just as the law brought the Hebrews.[10]

Clement thus offers one strategy for the Christian to view philosophy positively—namely, to consider it part of God's providential, missional work in the world.

A few centuries later St. Augustine (354–430 CE) would draw an analogy between gleaning the best fruit philosophy has to offer and the Hebrew people's plundering of Egypt on their way out of town (Ex 12:35-36). Gold is gold wherever you find it. The same goes for truth. Its value lies not in its source but in itself. If Christians find truth in an unlikely place, they ought not deny it but instead bring it to light and make use of it. In fact, it is plausible that such points of agreement among believers and nonbelievers could facilitate evangelism. In book VII of his autobiographical work, *Confessions*, Augustine carefully shows how in the writings of certain pagan philosophers he discovered many true insights that were compatible with the claims of Scripture. Interweaving quotations from the Gospel of John, he writes, "Again I found in them [the writings of the Neo-Platonic philosophers] that the Word, God, was *born not of flesh nor of blood, nor of the will of man nor of the will of the flesh, but of God* [John 1:13]; but I did not find that *the Word became flesh* [John 1:14]."[11] Rather than holding philosophers' views in suspicion simply because they come from philosophers, Augustine, like Clement, begins with the assumption that God desires to reveal his truth to all people.[12] Therefore, to some extent all people—even those who have not heard the gospel of Jesus Christ—are capable of discovering some God-revealed truth, perhaps especially those genuinely motivated by the pursuit of truth and wisdom.

To summarize, Clement believes philosophy might be the method by which God seeks to reach certain people with the gospel. Augustine believes that Christians should recognize all truth as God's truth, regardless

---

[10]Clement, in McGrath, *Christian Theology Reader*, 4-5.

[11]Augustine, *Confessions*, trans. F. J. Sheed, ed. Michael P. Foley (Indianapolis: Hackett, 2006), 127, emphasis original.

[12]Logicians refer to the error of reasoning in which one rejects an idea not because of the idea but because of its source as the genetic fallacy. There are good logical and theological reasons to try to avoid this sort of erroneous thinking.

of where it is found. A third response to the concerns about philosophy expressed above involves thinking more carefully about what philosophy is in the first place. While there is little agreement among present-day philosophers about its meaning, the classical definition of philosophy can be discerned through a literal translation from the Greek: "the love of wisdom." Even in the earliest days of philosophy in fifth-century BCE Greece, there were distinctions made between philosophers and others called Sophists, who appeared to be interested in wisdom but quite clearly were motivated instead by power, money, fame or simply winning arguments. Socrates, the father of Western philosophy, viewed philosophy and his own vocation as persuading his fellow citizens to care for virtue and to live life in accordance with justice, even if such a life would lead to persecution and death, as was the case with his own life. Obviously, given aims (and outcomes) like these, one can see why Clement and Augustine might have viewed philosophy not as a threat but as a worthwhile pursuit.

Turning to the later medieval, modern and contemporary philosophical worlds, the view of philosophy's compatibility with Christianity and with religion, more broadly, changes rather dramatically. In the medieval period nearly every Western philosopher was either Christian, Jew or Muslim, and thus very few questioned the compatibility of monotheistic faith and philosophical inquiry. In the modern period (seventeenth to nineteenth centuries), increasing tension between Christian faith and philosophy began to mount, so that by the early twentieth century, the few theistic philosophers left in the West seem quite reticent to disclose their theism. Despite this trajectory, in the last fifty years, and for a variety of reasons, Christian philosophy—and with it, the idea that faith and philosophy are compatible pursuits—has risen from the ashes. The thirty-five-year-old Society of Christian Philosophers has more than one thousand members, ranking it among the largest groups in the secular American Philosophical Association (APA). Christian philosophers have contributed not only to the subdiscipline of "philosophy of religion," but to all areas of philosophy, and no less than seven Christian philosophers have been honored as divisional president of the APA. Nowadays many, if not most, philosophers would reject the view that philosophy's primary activity is seeking wisdom.

Like many other academic disciplines in the West, over the past century there has been increasing specialization and intensified focus on particular areas of a discipline. As a result, many philosophers view their work as pursuing very particular lines of inquiry and seeking answers to very particular sorts of questions. Nevertheless, regardless of how one defines philosophy, it is quite clear that a growing number of confessing Christians believe they have been called to take part in the ongoing quests of philosophy, bringing salt and light to a community of people who desire truth and knowledge and in some cases, wisdom.

SHOULD THE CHRISTIAN BE SUSPICIOUS OF KIERKEGAARD?

Clearly there are good reasons to withhold suspicion about philosophy, generally speaking, but what about Kierkegaard, in particular? There are three kinds of concerns the Christian might have about a philosopher like Kierkegaard. First, one might wonder what the philosopher believes. Is the philosopher orthodox? Are the philosopher's theological views liberal or conservative? Could some of the philosopher's views be considered heretical? Second, one might be concerned less about the philosopher's own religious beliefs and more about the philosophy itself. Does the philosophical thought reflect traditional Christian teaching? Does it edify the church, or does it distract or point away from genuine Christian faith? Is it little more than a cultural product of its time? Third, stepping back from the philosopher and his or her work, one might wonder whether to bother inquiring after the thought of a philosopher given the attention his or her work has received from non-Christian sources. This is a worry of the "guilt by association" variety. If those who are *not* committed to Christ and his church value such-and-such a thinker, the reasoning goes, then there's got to be something un-Christian about him, something that might threaten the integrity of the Christian. Each of these three types of concern has surfaced in the criticism of Kierkegaard's thought by a handful of contemporary Christian thinkers. Some have questioned his Christianity—his personal views and practice, others the Christian direction of his work, and still others the alleged consequences of his writings visible in later philosophical and theological viewpoints.

How might one respond to these sorts of concerns? In the first case, as some evangelical critics have pointed out, Kierkegaard never writes the following: "Here exactly is what I believe about God: . . ." The truth is that most people don't. If one trolls around Kierkegaard's work long enough, particularly his own voluminous collection of journals, worries about Kierkegaard's own Christian faith dissipate rather quickly. Some of these confessional entries will be quoted below, so I will not say much more about this now. Suffice it to say there is no reason to think his personal Christian beliefs were outside the parameters of classic Reformed, Lutheran orthodoxy.

The second concern is whether Kierkegaard's work itself can be considered Christian in terms of its content and purpose. Does it encourage the reader to draw closer toward Christ? There are two ways to answer this question. The most obvious is to recognize its subjective nature and to ask those who've spent significant time reading Kierkegaard whether they've grown in faith (see, for example, "A Personal Story" in the introduction). Answers here will likely vary widely and be little more than anecdotal. If one seeks a slightly more objective response to this question, one could examine Kierkegaard's own understanding of what his authorship aims to do. If his own opinion counts for something, then in the very least one can rest assured that Kierkegaard's intentions are themselves consistent with Christian faith, whether or not his execution is successful. In one of the many places he reflects on the religious aims of his writings, he describes the purpose of his authorship as presenting "the ideal picture of being a Christian . . . so that it can crush with all its weight the presumptuousness of wanting to go further than being a Christian" (PV 130-31). Again, as with the first concern, it seems this second concern about the purpose of Kierkegaard's writings can be met successfully.

What about the third worry, arguably the most common, that given Kierkegaard's associations with secular philosophies and liberal theologies of the twentieth century, we can reason backwards and conclude that we ought to be suspicious of Kierkegaard? Importantly, this position rests on a logical error that goes something like this: because person x likes person y, and I believe person x to be wrong, I can safely assume person y is therefore wrong. This argument form is fallacious and implies something like the following:

1. The famous evolutionary biologist and outspoken atheist Richard Dawkins likes Jesus.[13]

2. I believe Dawkins's aggressive atheism to be wrong.

3. Therefore, I can safely assume Jesus is wrong.

Clearly this is faulty reasoning. What it suggests is that one ought to be apprehensive about dismissing thinkers based on who finds them appealing (and who does not). Instead one ought to attend to the thinkers and their writings themselves.

Let us turn for a moment to two examples of critical readings of Kierkegaard by evangelical voices from the past few decades. First, I will examine Dave Breese's discussion of Kierkegaard in *Seven Men Who Rule the World from the Grave* (1990), which I've selected primarily because it was published by an influential evangelical publishing company, Moody Press. Second, I will review the thought of the well-known apologist and pastor Francis Schaeffer. Schaeffer, many would agree, is among the most influential evangelical thinkers over the past half-century. Both, I argue, present incomplete and at times inaccurate pictures of Kierkegaard's philosophical ideas, and as a consequence, they mistake and underestimate his potential contribution to the lives of Christians. I take their views to be representative of many, though certainly not all popular evangelical thinkers.

Breese devotes one chapter each to seven figures—Darwin, Marx, Wellhausen, Dewey, Freud, Keynes and Kierkegaard—he believes have had a lasting and dangerous influence on contemporary Western thought and culture. The copy on the back cover of the book notes how these thinkers "generated philosophies that have been ardently grasped by masses of people but are erroneous and anti-scriptural." Breese's actual discussion of Kierkegaard's thought is rather brief—four pages on my count. The majority of the chapter on Kierkegaard is devoted to recounting the historical factors that preceded Kierkegaard's thought,

---

[13]See Richard Dawkins, "Atheists for Jesus," www.rationalresponders.com/atheists_for_jesus_a_richard_dawkins_essay, accessed August 15, 2015.

commentary on existentialism by a prominent philosopher, and the relationship between existentialism and twentieth-century theology.[14] In
his discussion of Kierkegaard Breese makes three troubling claims. The
first pertains not so much to the content of Kierkegaard's thought but
rather its effect on the reader. Breese finds Kierkegaard confusing, feels
that this is more or less the consensus viewpoint, and suspects that confusion is Kierkegaard's intended aim. Second, in highlighting the importance of the concept of passion in Kierkegaard's thought, Breese concludes after a two-paragraph discussion: "many of Kierkegaard's
interpreters suggest that he seems to be saying that passion is everything."[15]
Breese's third claim about Kierkegaard's thought really is about its effect
on future philosophy and theology, which he calls one of "diffusion." Diffusion, it appears, follows on the coattails of the confusion he believes
Kierkegaard conveyed to his reader, to the point that Kierkegaard embraced multiple, contradictory points of view. The diffusion Kierkegaard's thought promotes results in the exaltation of irrationality and
feeling, according to Breese.

    If Breese's criticisms of Kierkegaard are accurate, then there may be
good reason to end our inquiry here. However, while each of the three
claims has some basis in Kierkegaard's writings, ultimately they lack
support, and consequently Breese's concerns are unfounded. Prior to
considering those, however, I must briefly address Breese's research
methodology. Unfortunately, Breese provides *no* evidence that he has
read Kierkegaard himself.[16] His four-page discussion of Kierkegaard's
thought relies on one secondary piece of scholarship, Walter Kaufmann's
work *Existentialism from Dostoevsky to Sartre*, and every quotation of
Kierkegaard's that appears is a quotation Breese draws from Kaufmann's
book. (In fact, Breese mistakes Kaufmann's subject headings for the titles
of Kierkegaard's works, e.g. "On His Mission.") There are a few problems
with choosing Kauffman's text as one's primary (let alone only) source of

---

[14]This five-page section follows the logic of guilt by association noted above, and thus I will not
    address it.

[15]Dave Breese, *Seven Men Who Rule the World from the Grave* (Chicago: Moody, 1990), 215.

[16]In an article published in *Christianity Today*, C. Stephen Evans writes that one "reason for the
    evangelical neglect of Kierkegaard is simple: We have not read his books." "A Misunderstood
    Reformer," *Christianity Today* 28, no. 13 (1984): 28.

information about Kierkegaard, particularly when it appears one has not read the primary material. First, Kaufmann's book is not about Kierkegaard but rather a particular philosophical movement, existentialism. A broader, more careful view of the thinker would likely be found in a monograph devoted solely to that thinker, say, an introductory book about Kierkegaard.[17] Second, the notion that Kierkegaard is the father of existentialism, let alone an existentialist—a clear assumption of Kaufmann's book—is itself highly questionable and disputed by many Kierkegaard scholars. Existentialism, though itself hard to nail down, seems to operate with a number of basic assumptions that Kierkegaard explicitly rejects. One of these assumptions is the maxim verbalized by Jean-Paul Sartre, "existence precedes essence." Among other things, this view entails that human life is defined not by something outside oneself but by an individual's free choices. What one chooses to do is what constitutes one's identity. Neither God, nor the state, nor nature defines the self. Yet, Kierkegaard rejects and even mocks this sort of view time after time. (We will see in chapter three that Kierkegaard affirms the biblical view that humans are image-bearers of God.) The person who espouses this kind of radical freedom he jokingly calls "a king without a country" (SUD 69). Thus Breese's sole piece of research on Kierkegaard offers an interpretation of the thinker one has good reason to mistrust.

A third worry about relying solely on Kaufmann's work pertains to Kaufmann himself. Kaufmann was a highly regarded philosopher and a specialist in Kierkegaard, and yet he was also an outspoken atheist. Kaufmann's atheism is no reason to reject his commentary on Kierkegaard, as I warned above (see note 12). However, given Kaufmann's personal disagreement with Kierkegaard's own religious beliefs, many of which Kierkegaard writes about at great lengths, it would seem reasonable and beneficial to, in the least, supplement one's investigation into Kierkegaard with the scholarship of one more sympathetic to Kierkegaard's Christian faith, particularly when one of the primary issues at hand is the toxic effect of Kierkegaard's thought on Christianity. The scholarship of Christian philosophers like C. Stephen Evans, Robert L.

---

[17]I recommend the introductions to Kierkegaard by C. Stephen Evans, M. Jamie Ferreira or Julia Watkin. See my suggestions for further reading on p. 165.

Perkins, Robert C. Roberts, Sylvia Walsh or Merold Westphal is, in Kierkegaard circles, more highly regarded secondary literature on Kierkegaard anyway.

Let us turn back, however, to Breese's claims. Does Kierkegaard intend to confuse his reader? Is passion everything? And can we describe Kierkegaard's philosophical thought as embroiled in contradiction and therefore promoting irrationality? There is no doubt that to some extent Kierkegaard does intend to confuse his reader, and Breese bases his claim on a journal entry where Kierkegaard writes that he intends to "create difficulties everywhere." In the entry from which the quotation comes, Kierkegaard remarks that others in his day had made things rather easy and that since he couldn't find anything else to make easy, he'd do the opposite: make things more difficult. If one can detect the humor here, then we can move beyond the surface to ask what confusion is he trying to cause—what difficulty does he wish to create? Is he creating difficulties just to fool around with people, or could there be some earnest purpose? What sorts of things have been made easy? In *Practice in Christianity* Kierkegaard writes—again with a dose of humor—that over centuries in Christendom, "one became a Christian without noticing it," that with regard to becoming a Christian "everything became as simple as pulling on one's socks" (35).[18] In other words, the claims of Christianity, "living and active" truth, as Hebrews 4:12 says, deteriorated into little more than the rote doctrine one must memorize to be confirmed. Rather than marveling at the great paradox that God became a human to save us from our sins, Christians simply *assumed* that belief, finding it trivial and almost easy to believe. The laxness characterizing the beliefs and lives of Kierkegaard's contemporaries leads him to ask indignantly,

> What does it mean . . . that all these thousands and thousands as a matter
> of course call themselves Christians! These many, many people, of whom
> by far the great majority, according to everything that can be discerned,

---

[18]As we will discuss shortly, for a variety of reasons Kierkegaard employed a dozen pseudonyms as authors of a good portion of his writings. He attributes this work to a pseudonym, Anti-Climacus, whose thought represents the ideal Christian perspective. Though he claims the pseudonyms' viewpoints should not be taken as his own, one can clearly see in many places, like this quotation, that Kierkegaard seems to agree with his pseudonyms. Thus, unless I have reason to think Kierkegaard disagrees with a pseudonym, I will credit Kierkegaard as author.

have their lives in entirely different categories, something one can as-
certain by the simplest observation! (PV 41)

It is to his surrounding culture and their religious complacency, therefore,
that we must understand what Kierkegaard means when he says he
wishes to create difficulties, to create confusion. Is not the Christian life
a bit more involved, a bit more rigorous than pulling on one's socks?
Kierkegaard writes at length about the task of loving God and loving
one's neighbor, and about suffering for the truth. Given the emphasis on
these features of the Christian life, one can therefore understand why and
how Kierkegaard aims to create difficulties for Christians who view their
religious commitment as little more than attending church twice a year
or saying "yes" to catechism queries.

What about Breese's concern that for Kierkegaard passion is everything? His brief discussion is underdeveloped, although we can get a
sense of his concern given his reference to a well-known, often misunderstood phrase belonging to one of Kierkegaard's pseudonymous authors,
"truth is subjectivity." Kierkegaard believes that Christianity's doctrinal
elements, beliefs Christians take to be true, entail particular kinds of
religious feelings—e.g., humble awareness of one's sin, love for one's
neighbor—as well as actions—suffering for the truth, the humble worship
of God and so on. Oftentimes, however, only the first aspect is emphasized by the church; "faith" is reduced to a list of beliefs—gone is the
emotional and active side of Christian existence. Given this situation,
Christians continue to believe certain truths about God, yet live their
lives, as he notes, "in other categories" (BA 103). What Kierkegaard felt
was missing in the Christianity of his day was passion, and thus he emphasizes its importance to Christian existence and especially one's relationship to God. What are faith, hope and love, Kierkegaard might ask
us, if not Christian passions? Despite this emphasis on passion or in-
wardness or the subjective side of Christian faith, Kierkegaard does not
denigrate or minimize Christian doctrines or what his pseudonym calls
objective truth. In fact, Kierkegaard *assumes* Christian truth to be true.
He simply takes seriously the biblical view that the faith that transforms
a human life reaches beyond the mind to one's heart, soul and strength—
to one's passions.

Breese's third concern pertains to what he calls the "diffusion" of Kierkegaard's thought, which he takes to include a number of contradictory points of view that consequently subordinate reason to irrationality. In pointing out multiple points of view Breese is likely alluding to Kierkegaard's pseudonymous technique, whereby he writes several works under the guise of a variety of pseudonyms and then several other works using his own name. What would motivate Kierkegaard to use such a method, and does this amount to self-contradiction and the subsequent denigration of reason or rationality? One of Kierkegaard's stated aims is to reintroduce Christianity into Christendom. In a sense Kierkegaard is a Christian missionary *to Christians*. This odd predicament necessitated, he believed, an indirect approach. If someone already believes he or she is a Christian, then the direct charge "you ought to become a Christian" will make little sense and likely offend or alienate one's audience.[19] So Kierkegaard decides he will take an indirect approach and provisionally grant his contemporaries their Christianity, and he will write some books from a non-Christian point of view with the hopes of generating introspection among the "Christians" of his day. So, for example, around the same time that he publishes several Scripture-based devotional writings called upbuilding discourses under his own name, he publishes a pseudonymous two-volume work called *Either/Or* that explores life from a non-Christian perspective (in volume one) and a culturally Christian perspective (in volume two).[20]

Reflecting back on this "dual-stream" of his authorship, Kierkegaard writes, "With my left hand I passed *Either/Or* out into the world, with my right hand *Two Upbuilding Discourses*; but they all or almost all took the left hand with their right" (PV 36). That is to say, his contemporaries, nearly all of whom would describe themselves as Christians, had much greater interest in the more entertaining, less serious and religiously rigorous writings. Through this unusual strategy Kierkegaard hoped to provoke "Christians" who were attracted more to the pseudonymous

---

[19]We will see in chapter four that Kierkegaard is not opposed to offense, far from it; however, he is careful to differentiate appropriate from inappropriate forms of Christian offense.

[20]The first volume displays the aesthetic sphere of existence, while the second displays the ethical sphere of existence. We will discuss the spheres of existence in detail in chapter three.

writings than the religious writings to self-reflect and take a hard, honest look at their own faith commitments. If one understands Kierkegaard's unusual methodology and sees its relation to the stated objectives of his authorship, then the contradictions of various pseudonyms' writings don't amount to actual contradictions on the part of Kierkegaard. They show that, in fact, certain worldviews and lifestyles are in tension or in contradiction with the Christian worldview and lifestyle, something anyone would grant.

What about the exaltation of irrationality over rationality? This leads us to Francis Schaeffer's interpretation of Kierkegaard. Schaeffer deserves enormous credit for his work across several decades modeling how biblical Christianity might engage the philosophical world of ideas, which has impacted how we all live. Schaeffer discusses Kierkegaard in a number of his well-known works, including *The God Who Is There*, *Escape from Reason* and *How Should We Then Live?* Given his historical survey approach to philosophy and theology, his primary interest in Kierkegaard is not so much Kierkegaard's thought as it is "Kierkegaardianism," as he calls it, or "Kierkegaardian existentialism" in both its secular and religious forms. I've given reason above to question and quite possibly reject the association of Kierkegaard with existentialism, so I will not repeat those objections again, and neither will I explore Schaeffer's claims that Kierkegaard's thought naturally leads to Camus, Sartre or, on the theological side, Karl Barth and Paul Tillich. In my estimation those claims rest on a variety of philosophical constructs that Schaeffer creates to show how we have arrived where we are in an age that has, for lack of better terms, lost its reason. Despite Schaeffer's commitment to tracing the movement of ideas through history, I find those constructs unconvincing and a bit too simplistic.

At the center of Kierkegaard's alleged existentialism and irrationality, according to Schaeffer, is the concept of the leap of faith, and in nearly every discussion of Kierkegaard across Schaeffer's works this concept is at the fore. Schaeffer is not alone in linking Kierkegaard primarily with the idea of a leap of faith. It is interesting to note, however, that the expression "leap of faith" *never* occurs in Kierkegaard's published work. Moreover, as Mariele Nientied claims, "the terms 'faith' and 'leap' rarely appear in the same contexts, nor do variants of these words."[21] If this is the case, then why does Schaeffer alongside esteemed philosophers like Alasdair Mac-Intyre view Kierkegaard as promoting a form of irrationalism?

One of the great projects of philosophy, dating from classical philosophers like Socrates and Zeno to modern thinkers like Hume and Kant, is the exploration of the limits of human reason. Philosophers have traditionally claimed that life ought to be guided primarily by reason (as opposed, say, to emotions), and yet only the insane or remarkably arrogant would believe that human reason is a faculty without limit. As a Lutheran Christian, Kierkegaard believed that human reason was limited not simply by cognitive constraints, but by our moral and spiritual shortcomings. Put in theological terms, human reason has been negatively affected by sin. Thus our limited ability to discover truth is not simply because we're not smart enough, but because we're not good enough—our character is deeply flawed. As a result Kierkegaard is highly critical of reason—not generally speaking, but when it takes the form of hubris or ethical and religious evasion, when it fails to recognize its limits. Merold Westphal captures Kierkegaard's view of the triumphal attitudes reason sometimes takes: "when human thought calls itself 'Reason,' this is all too often little more than self-capitulation and even self deception."[22] Philosophers, Kierkegaard and St. Augustine would suggest, are experts at using reason in the service of putting off commitment and service to others and to God. After all, the philosopher can always develop more arguments, raise more objections, introduce more considerations, ad nauseam. *Why don't we keep talking, keep thinking, so long as we don't actually have to do anything!*

Kierkegaard is highly critical of this tendency for excessive reflectiveness in philosophy, which sets the stage for his use of the concept of the leap. Leap primarily refers to the "category of decision" (CUP 99), whereby one chooses, for example, to trust God, just as the old hymn

---

[21]Mariele Nientied, "Kierkegaard Without 'Leap of Faith,'" in *Pre-Proceedings of the 26th International Wittgenstein Symposium* (Austrian Ludwig Wittgenstein Society, Kirchberg am Wechsel, 2003), 263.

[22]Merold Westphal, *Whose Community? Which Interpretation?: Philosophical Hermeneutics for the Church* (Grand Rapids: Baker Academic, 2009), 151. See also Westphal's *Kierkegaard's Critique of Reason and Society* (Macon, GA: Mercer University Press, 1987).

goes, "I have decided to follow Jesus." It is important to see that trusting God in just this way is not a decision one makes because God's existence has been philosophically proven. But it does not follow from this that when one places trust in God one does so for *no* reason or *without* reason or necessarily *against* reason. Schaeffer accuses Kierkegaard of not reading the Bible carefully enough because when he recounts the story of Abraham's binding of Isaac in his work *Fear and Trembling*, he said it was "an act of faith with nothing rational to base it upon or to which to relate it."[23] According to Schaeffer, Kierkegaard failed to acknowledge that Abraham's actions are not irrational given that he had seen and heard from God, that "God's words at this time were in the context of Abraham's strong reason for knowing that God both existed and was totally trustworthy."[24] Unfortunately, Schaeffer's criticism here misses the mark and trades on a bit of equivocation.

As it turns out, Kierkegaard is well aware of the biblical story of Abraham, quoting constantly from Scripture in his retelling of Abraham's obedience to God. In fact, Schaeffer's criticism that Kierkegaard emphasizes faith over reason in discussing Abraham really seems a critique not of Kierkegaard but of the author of Hebrews 11. Following the refrain of Hebrews 11, Kierkegaard repeatedly introduces the events in Abraham's life that climaxed in the binding of Isaac by showing how these occurred "by faith." "By faith Abraham emigrated from the land of his fathers and became a foreigner in the promised land," Kierkegaard writes. "By faith Abraham received the promise that in his seed all the generations of the world would be blessed" (FT 14). Emphasizing faith in this context seems biblically and—from a Reformed perspective— theologically correct. It seems that when Schaeffer speaks of reason or rationality in the context of Abraham, he is using it in the everyday sense in which we say one has a reason for doing this or that. Of course, using this everyday sense of reason, sociopaths have reasons for their actions, even though we would question their rationality. It goes without saying that Abraham obeys God's command to sacrifice Isaac *for the*

---

[23]Francis Schaeffer, *The God Who Is There*, in *The Complete Works of Francis Schaeffer* (Westchester, IL: Crossway Books, 1982), 1:15.
[24]Ibid., 15-16.

reason that he believes in God, trusts God, has a history with God fulfilling his promises and so on. But saying Abraham has good *reason* to follow God—something with which Kierkegaard would heartily agree—is a far cry from calling Abraham's obedience "rational." It seems at that point rationality becomes a matter of perspective and needs some precise definition. From the perspective of those who do not believe in God, or who believe child sacrifice to be universally prohibited—something Abraham's descendants would come to believe—Abraham's obedience seems irrational. This is why Kierkegaard calls Abraham's obedience absurd. Is his obedience absurd or irrational from the perspective of faith? Of course not; Abraham is the paragon of faith. But if one is willing to recognize and then sympathize with other vantage points—even vantage points one believes to be incorrect—one can see why others would view such an action as absurd or irrational.

I conclude, therefore, that the concept of the leap of faith—a concept far less important to Kierkegaard's work than many think—does not entail irrationality at all. Schaeffer's grandiose claims that follow this assessment—that after Kierkegaard "one must try to find meaning without reason" or one must give up "hope of a unity of knowledge and a unity of life" and remain content with "a fragmented concept of reality"—do not follow at all.[25] For a decisive refutation of the alleged irrationality of Kierkegaard, I commend C. Stephen Evans's "Is Kierkegaard an Irrationalist?"[26] I conclude this section by quoting Evans's 1984 article on Kierkegaard in *Christianity Today*: "Poor Kierkegaard has suffered more than any author I know of from a generation of evangelical ignorance."[27]

WHO IS KIERKEGAARD THE THINKER?

Unlike Breese and Schaeffer, a number of present-day Christian scholars, preachers and authors have drawn inspiration from Kierkegaard's thought. I have already mentioned several Christian philosophers. Presbyterian pastor Timothy Keller and popular author Philip Yancey have

---

[25]Schaeffer, *How Should We Then Live?* in *Complete Works*, 5:179, 199. Schaeffer thankfully concedes, "There can and will be a continuing discussion among scholars as to whether the secular and religious thinkers who built on Kierkegaard did him justice" (ibid., 179).

[26]C. Stephen Evans, "Is Kierkegaard an Irrationalist?" *Religious Studies* 25 (1989): 347-62.

[27]C. Stephen Evans, "A Misunderstood Reformer," *Christianity Today*, September 21, 1984, 28.

both made use of Kierkegaard's thought in their preaching and writing, respectively.[28] In the remainder of the chapter I would like to expand on how these others have benefited from Kierkegaard's thought. Though to this point I have focused on Kierkegaard as a philosopher, here I will cast his thought more broadly and point to the many "hats" he wears, which explains his wide appeal to scholars of different disciplines. These hats, many of which he seems to wear concurrently, include philosopher, theologian, biblical interpreter, psychologist, prophet, missionary and poet.

Philosopher. We have already seen how philosophy might serve some good if it is devoted to wisdom. There is no doubt that Kierkegaard valued this aspect of classical philosophical inquiry, leading Robert C. Roberts to comment, "The project behind Kierkegaard's authorship is the increase of Christian wisdom."[29] Another fundamental practice of philosophy (and especially classical philosophy) is the art of conceptual analysis: the examination, investigation and clarification of a variety of concepts. Nearly every pre-Socratic philosopher was preoccupied with investigating what made the cosmos or the world tick; their analysis concerned the Greek concept of *logos*. It is with this tradition of reasoning in mind that the Gospel writer John *identifies* Jesus with *logos*; *logos* was a philosophically loaded term he used intentionally for evangelistic purposes. Conceptual analysis is also central to Plato's writing in the form of dialogues. Most often the dialogues center on the following kind of question: "What is ___?," thereby aiming to provide clarity and understanding of concepts like knowledge, courage or piety.

Kierkegaard himself is an analyst of concepts with unquestionable skill and precision, leading Roberts to call him a conceptual surgeon who engages in conceptual therapy. At the center of conceptual analysis is the activity of making careful distinctions between concepts that resemble each other, including those that share a name. Everyone can relate to phrases like the following: there's barbecue and then there's barbecue; or there's beautiful and then there's beautiful. Kierkegaard was fond of this sort of refrain—there's love and then there's love, for example. In

---

[28]Keller titles a sermon after one of Kierkegaard's books, *The Sickness unto Death.*
[29]Robert C. Roberts, "The Philosopher as Sage: A Review Essay," *Journal of Religious Ethics* 22, no. 2 (Fall 1994): 416.

exploring the fine distinctions between competing conceptions of ideas like love, offense, Christian and faith—all of which we examine in this book—Kierkegaard's writing exemplifies philosophical virtues such as clarity, thoroughness and tenacity.

Despite his commitment to wisdom and his excellence in analyzing concepts, some have claimed that Kierkegaard does not deserve the title philosopher. One of the twentieth century's most famous philosophers, Bertrand Russell, makes not a single mention of Kierkegaard in his almost nine-hundred-page history of Western philosophy. In a qualified sense Russell may be right; Kierkegaard himself would probably concede he's at least not a philosopher's philosopher. That is, he does not concern himself with theory construction, or developing a grand system of thought, or speculating for speculation's sake. And of course Russell was, famously, an outspoken atheist, writing at a time when Christian philosophy was subterranean if it existed at all, and thus Kierkegaard's primary interest in religious faith was likely a turnoff to Russell. Not much hinges on labeling Kierkegaard a philosopher since the term itself is nearly impossible for philosophers themselves to define with any sort of consensus. Nevertheless, it should be emphasized that the rigor with which Kierkegaard thinks about a variety of topics central to human life exhibits a strong commitment both to wisdom and to intellectual excellence.

Theologian and biblical interpreter. Although Kierkegaard had theological and seminary training, he is not usually considered a theologian as much as a religious philosopher. Nevertheless, one finds in his work lengthy discussions of doctrines central to the Christian faith, including God, Jesus Christ, sin, atonement, the church, salvation and justification. Interacting with the theology of the church fathers, the Reformers and his own contemporaries, Kierkegaard makes no mistake that his interests revolve not around crafting a new systematic theology or church dogmatics but thinking through doctrines and Scripture in such a way that his contemporaries might be challenged to hear the gospel anew and live accordingly. In a sense it would be appropriate to describe Kierkegaard's as a practical theology.

At the end of his monumental philosophical work *Concluding Unscientific Postscript*, he offers comment about the purpose of his pseudonyms that sheds light on his theological and biblical interests:

> Their importance . . . unconditionally does not consist in making any new proposal, some unheard-of discovery, or in founding a new party and wanting to go further, but precisely in the opposite, in wanting to have no importance, in wanting, at a remove that is the distance of double-reflection, once again to read through solo, if possible in a more inward way, the original text of individual human existence-relationships, the old familiar text handed down from the fathers. (CUP 629-30)

Kierkegaard is, of course, speaking about the Bible, and the sentiment reflected in this quotation is what I call Kierkegaard's "nothing new policy." Contrary to some of the interpretations of Christians and non-Christians alike, fundamentally Kierkegaard offers nothing new in terms of his theological vision of the biblical view of human life. We will discuss below Kierkegaard's deep exploration of a variety of different life-views, different ways people think about and carry out their existence. As we can see from the quotation, Kierkegaard believes that the Bible speaks directly to this very human question, and that Christian existence itself is the highest life-view, the most optimal (though not the easiest) way to live one's life.

Perhaps, then, it is fair to regard Kierkegaard as a theologian only in that he takes the traditional theology of the church and attempts to present it is a new, practical and fresh way, one that will cultivate proper understanding of and passion for the Christian life. Or as he puts it,

> Through my writing I hope to achieve the following: to leave behind me so accurate a characterization of Christianity and its relationships in the world that an enthusiastic, noble-minded young person will be able to find in it a map of relationships as accurate as any topographical map from the most famous institutes. (JP 6:77-78 [#6283])

Psychologist. The quote above leads naturally to another hat Kierkegaard wears: psychologist. Psychology as we now know it—the modern discipline with which we associate figures like Freud, Jung and Erikson—did not yet exist during Kierkegaard's lifetime. Freud was born the year following Kierkegaard's death. And yet two of Kierkegaard's books published in the 1840s include variations of the word *psychological*, and nearly every work in some way explores the contours of human existence. Modern psychology credits Kierkegaard for his early insights into the depth psychology that Freud and others would develop and eventually make mainstream. Depth psychology explores the multiple layers of the self beyond the conscious level to ask how issues beneath the surface might inform who we are and who we take ourselves to be in everyday life. This may sound kooky to those not sympathetic to modern psychology, but those familiar with Scripture may recognize that Kierkegaard's penetration of the self is not novel. One could argue, for example, that St. Paul is putting his finger on the unconscious when he writes, "I do not understand my own actions. For I do not do what I want, but I do the very thing I hate" (Rom 7:15). Besides depth psychology, Kierkegaard also explores what psychologists today would call developmental psychology, in his formulation of the spheres of existence—aesthetic, ethical and religious—to be explored at length in chapter three.

Psychologist and theologian Eric Johnson calls Kierkegaard the "father of Christian psychology" because Kierkegaard so helpfully explores the Christian view of what it means to be human and how that view relates to and contrasts with other perspectives. In particular, Kierkegaard discerns the multifarious ways our need and desire for God get hijacked by our will *not* to be who God created us to be. Many of us want to decide who we will become, repeating Frank Sinatra's standard American hero mantra, "I did it my way." Others of us, perhaps shrouded in self-loathing and guilt, don't believe that in our sorry state God can improve us. We wish to avoid being the self God created us to be not out of an open desire to be in charge but because we don't think we're quality material for transformation. Kierkegaard's psychology is comprehensive in its diagnosis of a variety of spiritual human ailments, but it is also nurturing and contains implications for counseling therapy.

Prophet and missionary. As a child I thought the sole mark of the biblical prophets was their ability to foretell the future. Perhaps this thinking flowed from hearing Isaiah's suffering servant passages (e.g., Is 53) read alongside the New Testament birth stories every Christmas. Prediction of future events is central to the office of prophet in Deuteronomy

18, which instructs Israel to distinguish a genuine prophet by his true predictions. There is a second, broader conception of a prophet present, however, in Exodus 7:1, where God tells Moses that Aaron will serve as his prophet to Pharaoh. Prophet in this case has nothing to do with predicting the future but with one person *speaking for* another. On this view prophets of God are fundamentally God's spokespersons who may deliver messages about the future but who may also bring words of encouragement or of condemnation for the present age. This broader sense of the term explains why, for instance, Martin Luther King Jr. or Gandhi have been called prophets. Their acclaim has come not through prediction but through conveying a divine message to backward cultures that needed to hear them.

To some small degree Kierkegaard seems to fill both prophetic roles. On the one hand, he seems to be aware that given the current trajectory of Christianity in Denmark and Europe, its future is bleak. Though he does not seem interested in prognostication, it is clear to him what the future holds, save a significant turnabout. Just prior to his attack on Christendom, Kierkegaard claims that Christianity has "become paganism," that "Christendom has abolished Christ" despite its attempt "to delude us into thinking that Christendom is Christ" (PC 107). Why Kierkegaard thinks these things to be true will be examined at great length in the course of the book, though one factor has already been addressed above—the arrogance of the established state church. "This deification of the established order is the perpetual revolt, the continual mutiny against God" (PC 88). Sadly, Kierkegaard would not be surprised at the church today. While nearly 80 percent of Denmark maintains membership in the established state church, just 3 percent regularly attend. Perhaps more disconcerting is that despite the membership rate, only 28 percent claim to believe in God.

The second sense of prophet pertains to speaking for God. Speaking for God is a dicey affair, as one reads in the book of Job. On the one hand, speaking for God is a terribly presumptuous and dangerous thing to do. It doesn't take much imagination to ponder our reaction to those who make such claims. *Who are you that you think you know what God wants?* Or, *How dare you claim to speak God's words?!* It is no wonder that prophets very often get killed for their proclamations—biblical prophets as well as King and Gandhi. On the other hand, Scripture commands not only that prophets but *all* followers of Christ speak for God, that is, serve as prophets. Matthew 28:19-20, the Great Commission of Christ, commands that God's words be told to those who have not heard them. Perhaps that is the distinguishing mark of the Old Testament prophet and the New Testament missionary: the prophet preaches primarily to the choir, preaches to Israel. The missionary preaches primarily to those outside the church, those who have not heard. Kierkegaard seems to be doing a little of both. Given his audience, which (1) identifies itself as Christian, (2) has knowledge of Christian doctrine and (3) attends church, his presentation of ideal Christianity—however indirect—seems prophetic in the Old Testament sense. And just as the prophets of God did not introduce new theology but simply repeated the same call and message God had given for generations and generations, so too is Kierkegaard's message of Christianity to Christians not conveying novel information. One might nevertheless think of Kierkegaard as he did himself, as a Christian missionary to Christians, insofar as the gospel his contemporaries have heard has not, in fact, been the gospel, but rather some familiar-sounding, speculative, philosophy-infused religious pep talk.

Poet. Kierkegaard believed that serving as a Christian missionary to Christians was a unique and challenging task requiring an unusual strategy: "an illusion can never be removed directly, and basically only indirectly" (PV 43). One feature of Kierkegaard's indirect methods of communication, then, was the poetic. In several places Kierkegaard describes himself as a "religious poet" or a "poet-dialectician." Though these terms are not synonymous, each conveys Kierkegaard's method of using colorful, lyrical speech and literary rather than philosophical genres to convey serious or earnest messages. At times Kierkegaard uses the term *poetic* to refer to an aesthetic style of writing or to the books he published pseudonymously. In the retrospective work *The Point of View* he makes two important claims about his use of the poetic. First, as a natural talent and gift of God, his poetic ability was on display from the beginning to end of the authorship despite the authorship's transition toward more explicitly Christian writing. Second, the poetic was all the time subservient to the religious. That is to say, besides calling himself a poet, Kierkegaard describes himself as a religious author, even in those works attributed to pseudonyms that describe nonreligious life-views. Kierkegaard openly confesses inner dialogues he repeatedly had that involve keeping the poetic in check, lest his ability to compose beautiful or clever prose overtake and override the message of the Christian ideal he felt called to convey.

The poetic thus serves the indirect method Kierkegaard believed was required by a Christianity-less Christendom. There is another reason he makes use of the poetic, one that stands regardless of his religious context. As we noted above, Kierkegaard felt strongly that Christianity amounts to more than a list of true propositions about God. Rather, Christianity concerns one's whole life, in particular one's heart and emotions. In Jesus' Sermon on the Mount (Mt 5–7) it is clear that the heart, and not simply outward obedience to rules, signifies one's love for God. "Blessed are the *meek*, the *pure in heart*, the *poor in spirit*." It is *not* "Blessed are those who believe true propositions about God, or those with sophisticated theology." When one is saved by Christ salvation comes to the whole self— the mind, but also the heart, soul and body. Kierkegaard describes Christianity as having a "pathos-filled" element. That is, to become a Christian involves feeling certain sorts of things—whether compassion for the poor in spirit or hope for the sufferer. The poetic, Kierkegaard believed, could touch deeply this pathos-filled core of the Christian faith better than didactic sermons or classroom lectures. Those who've been moved by a favorite hymn or song can speak to the power of the poetic to convey Christian sentiment as well as Christian doctrine. Thus one finds in many of Kierkegaard's writings (and especially his prayers) not poetry itself, but a poetic style of communication that stirs the soul and speaks to the heart.

Perhaps these numerous hats explain why commentators of Kierkegaard have interpreted him in such a diverse number of ways. Yet, as I have argued elsewhere, however one reads Kierkegaard, through whatever discipline one wishes to do so, one cannot in good faith ignore his Christian commitments and the degree to which he envisions his authorship as serving God by making use of his particular talents and gifts.[30] The Christian reader will find no difficulty with this claim given the writings and ideas of Kierkegaard we will now explore.

QUESTIONS FOR REFLECTION

1. Do I tend to accept or seriously consider ideas more because of their content or their source/author? Does this help or hurt me in finding God's truth?

2. Am I suspicious of ideas that do not come from Scripture or Christian sources, and if so, why?

---

[30]Mark A. Tietjen, *Kierkegaard, Communication, and Virtue: Authorship as Edification* (Bloomington: Indiana University Press, 2013).

JESUS CHRIST

*Blessed is the one who knows of no one else to go to
but in everything knows how to go to him.*

PRACTICE IN CHRISTIANITY, 75

CHRISTIANS HAVE LONG HELD that there is no question more fundamental to their faith, no question with more at stake, than "Who is Jesus?" In his first letter to the Corinthians the apostle Paul admits that if his basic understanding of Jesus is wrong, then all is for naught; "if Christ has not been raised, then our proclamation has been in vain and your faith has been in vain" (1 Cor 15:14). Of course, not everyone in the world sees Jesus the same way. A few years ago I attended a large book festival near Atlanta and was struck by a sign on a booth that read, "Islam: The way of Adam, Noah, Abraham, Moses, and Jesus." I imagine most passersby who noticed the sign were startled by the inclusion on this list of those Jewish and Christian patriarchs, but especially the inclusion of Jesus. Hindus, too, hold Jesus in a positive light, considering him to be a reincarnation of the god Krishna. Even some atheists (Richard Dawkins— yes; Bertrand Russell—not so much) have offered approving commentary. Who knew that Jesus' approval rating was so high! Amid all of these odd affirmations a Christian may understandably ask just how exactly these various groups conceive of Jesus. Is he the turn-the-other-cheek pacifist Jesus? Or the defy-religious-authority rebel Jesus? Or the parable-telling sage Jesus? Or the Son of God, Savior-of-the-world Jesus?

Confusion and disagreement about Jesus' identity are nothing new but can be found throughout church history, dating back as far as the New Testament. The Gospels record Jesus surveying his disciples about popular opinion: "Who do people say that I am?" The question is poignant enough for Jesus then to turn it directly to the disciples: "Who do *you* say that I am?" On Jesus' arrest, the high priest inquires: "Are you the Messiah, the Son of the Blessed One?" And all four Gospels record Pilate's interrogation: "Are you the king of the Jews?" This sampling suggests that for the Gospel writers Jesus' identity was of chief importance. Was he who he claimed to be? Was he who others thought he was? It is no small matter whether Jesus is no more than a member of a long line of prophets, as Islam proposes, or he is the reincarnation of Krishna, as Hinduism posits, or he is one of a handful of truly enlightened souls, as Buddhism posits, or he is God in flesh, as the classical Christian tradition has maintained. Given the wide range of conflicting claims about Jesus as well as the varied implications of these claims for human lives, the issue of Jesus' identity still demands thoughtfulness and earnest reflection today.

Living in a far less pluralistic society than our own, Kierkegaard was not at all concerned with how Muslims, Hindus or atheists understood Jesus. He was interested instead in what his Christian contemporaries thought, and his conviction was that many of them held *unchristian* views. These views, which involve an idiosyncratic understanding of Jesus and also of his role in salvation, include the following:

1. *The "liberal theology" view.*[1] Liberal theology, in its infancy during Kierkegaard's life, questioned traditional Christian understandings of sin and the divinity of Jesus. If the doctrine of sin is fundamentally mistaken or, in the least, overstated, then the need for a savior *from sin* diminishes. Therefore the notion that Jesus is truly God—an archaic belief thought to be untenable in the modern world—is far from necessary, since savior-work is no longer necessary. Jesus can still inspire one toward living a better, more moral life, but the notion of salvation from sin loses its utility.

---

[1]The names for each view are my own, not Kierkegaard's.

2. ***The "Pelagian" view.*** This understanding of Jesus gets its name from the fourth-century heretic Pelagius, who was notorious for claiming that humans can contribute to their salvation. Those who conceive of Jesus in this way minimize the sufficiency of his death and resurrection for human salvation and thereby sell short the centrality of grace in salvation. This view promotes what Scripture sometimes refers to as works-righteousness.

3. ***The "grace-abuse" view.*** Opposite the Pelagian view, grace abuse converts teaching about God's grace in Jesus Christ into license to act with little consideration for God's law or call to holiness. The grace abuser believes that Jesus' perfect life—while efficacious for salvation—is not something that can be emulated, and therefore it is not something *to be* emulated. Grace abusers are those Paul has in mind when he writes, "What then are we to say? Should we continue in sin in order that grace may abound?" (Rom 6:1).

Each of these mistaken views concerning the nature of salvation and Jesus' role therein remains in play in today's world. Oddly enough, the first position can be found among atheists and believers alike. If—as I previously made my living—one hangs around secular university campuses long enough, one can find any number of people who think positively of Jesus but would never consider themselves Christian, would never view him as divine Savior. The liberal theological view also remains prevalent in many mainline churches and seminaries today. Within the walls of many if not most churches one finds the other two positions in their contemporary variations—those who, knowingly or not, believe and act as though their goodness or intelligence merits God's favor, and those who fail to view Jesus as a model of holy living to be imitated.

In what follows we will explore the ways Kierkegaard critiques these problematic theologies, attending also to how they may be manifest in our own ways of thinking and living. We will consider his correctives of each view: Jesus Christ as the God-human, the sufficient savior and the pattern, respectively. We conclude the chapter with one further image of Jesus as gentle savior.

GOD-HUMAN

> Jesus isn't lettin' you off the hook. The Scriptures don't let you off the hook
> so easily. . . . When people say, you know, "Good teacher," "Prophet,"
> "Really nice guy" . . . this is not how Jesus thought of Himself. So you're
> left with a challenge in that . . . either Jesus was who he said he was or a
> complete and utter nut case. . . . You have to make a choice on that. And
> I believe that Jesus was, you know, the Son of God. And I understand that
> . . . we need to be really, really respectful to people who find that ridiculous
> and . . . preposterous.[2]

These are the words of Paul Hewson, AKA Bono, lead singer of the
Irish rock band U2 and outspoken Christian humanitarian, though
(with a bit of polishing) they could be the words of C. S. Lewis or
Kierkegaard.[3] In *Mere Christianity* Lewis presents his famous "tri-
lemma" argument, in which he claims it is irrational to view Jesus as
many of his contemporaries viewed him—as a good moral teacher, a
guru, a wise man comparable to the Buddha or Confucius.[4] In light
of the claims of Scripture—Jesus' words about himself, others' words
about him and Jesus' actions—Lewis believed that such a position
was unfounded and based more on wishful thinking than solid evidence. If one grants the "Jesus as moral teacher" position is unsound,
Lewis concludes, one is left with just three choices: he is a lunatic, a
liar ("the Devil of Hell") or the Lord. Those who prefer to view Jesus
as moral teacher would clearly reject the first two options and thus
must face directly the claim that so deeply offends—that Jesus is Lord.
The argument has received much attention and criticism, and although Lewis himself would have been the first to admit that his
scholarly strengths lay not primarily in philosophical argument,
many continue to find the argument compelling.

---

[2]Jeremy Weber, "Six Surprises from Bono's Interview with Focus on the Family," *Gleanings* (blog),
June 21, 2013, www.christianitytoday.com/gleanings/2013/june/bono-interview-with-focus-on
-family-jim-daly.html.
[3]See C. S. Lewis, *Mere Christianity* (New York: HarperSanFrancisco, 2001), 52; and Søren Kierkegaard, "[In] Christendom we have all become Christians without perceiving any possibility of
offense at an individual human being's speaking and acting in terms of being God" (PC 102).
[4]In a less developed form, the argument appears also at the end of the first chapter of *The Problem
of Pain.*

Kierkegaard never understood his own writing as a kind of Christian apologetic, in part because his audience—unlike Lewis's—had not yet begun to admit it found the biblical claims doubtful.[5] However, Kierkegaard makes a very similar argument to Lewis's approximately one hundred years earlier, directing his reasoning *toward Christians* who might be inclined to conceive of Jesus as something less than God incarnate, than the God-human, as he puts it. He takes up the issue most directly in *Philosophical Fragments*, which explores the idea that God became human and offers humans eternal happiness and salvation. *Fragments* itself is hardly direct, however. It is a pseudonymous writing, for one, and it is written in a very unusual, somewhat playful form. One scholar refers to part of the book as a mock deduction of Christianity insofar as the pseudonymous author, Johannes Climacus, constructs a thought experiment with an unlikely, even offensive conclusion.[6] I will describe the thought experiment below, but the offensive conclusion is nothing more than the truth of the basic Christian story. Why, one might wonder, would the truth of Christianity be offensive to an ostensibly Christian audience? As it turns out, the offensiveness of the argumentation pertains not to the Christian truth it affirms, but instead to *how* those truths are established, the basis on which they seem to be true. By way of analogy, there is nothing offensive about my wife claiming she loves me—in fact I strongly believe it to be true. But if she said she loved me because of how I dressed I would be offended, though not at her love for me but how she arrived at that love.

Before delving further into the offensiveness of the argument, however, let us back up a bit. *Fragments* begins with the questions of (1) *whether* one can learn truth, and if so (2) *how* one learns truth, a line of inquiry that Kierkegaard's pseudonym openly borrows from Socrates, who discusses the topic in one of Plato's dialogues. (As with Jesus, all we know of Socrates comes from a handful of other Greeks, including most importantly Plato, his pupil.) His methodology runs as follows: at every turn in the argument, Climacus clearly states what he takes to be the Socratic answer to the particular

---

[5]We will explore Kierkegaard's views of offense at Jesus and the topic of apologetics in chapter four.

[6]See Robert C. Roberts, *Faith, Reason, and History: Rethinking Kierkegaard's* Philosophical Fragments (Macon, GA: Mercer University Press, 1986).

question posed and then he wonders aloud—what would a view opposite the Socratic look like? So, for example, if when looking for truth, Socrates claims, one can find it within oneself, then the opposite view would simply be something like "truth can be found only outside oneself." What the reader quickly discovers is that the opposite view in every move of the argument strongly resembles the Christian perspective, though Christianity is not explicitly named. Perhaps one might begin to see how the alert Christian reader might be offended by Climacus's method of deriving a view of things that appears an awful lot like Christianity. For he seems *through human reason and logic* to be deriving or establishing the truth of Christian doctrine. Why is this a problem? What makes such methodology offensive? One of the fundamental beliefs of Protestant Christianity is that its truth is revealed by God alone. No human mind could ever deduce Christianity logically; Christianity, every Danish child should know, did not arise in a human heart. Rather, it is *revealed* religion.

Though it undoubtedly defies present-day views of what counts as funny to call this sort of philosophical writing humorous, Kierkegaard wants his reader in the very least to smirk to him- or herself and not simply be offended. Every reader of his day knew two things just as confidently as they knew what they ate for breakfast. First, they *knew* God became a human being in the incarnation of Jesus of Nazareth. Second, they *knew* this to be true *because* God revealed it in Scripture, *not* through logic and argument. The problem, as Kierkegaard sees it, is subtle and lies in the word *know*. In "knowing" that God took on flesh and entered human history, the belief had become trivial, rote and passé. Lost on Kierkegaard's contemporaries is the fact that this claim they *know* as easily and confidently as they *know* they ate scrambled eggs and toast could seem "ridiculous and preposterous," as Bono puts it, to those who do not *know*. In another work Kierkegaard writes,

> In an inadmissible and illicit way we have become "knowing" about Christ—for the admissible way is to become "believing." We have mutually fortified one another in the thought that by means of the outcome of Christ's life and the eighteen hundred years, by means of the results we have come to know the answer. As this gradually became wisdom, *all the vitality and energy was distilled out of Christianity.* (PC 35, emphasis mine)

Kierkegaard, through a bit of intellectual playfulness, is trying to apply a bit of doctrinal shock treatment to parroting Christians who almost involuntarily spout Christianese without (1) recognizing how counter and offensive Christian beliefs are to those who do not hold them and (2) allowing the life-transforming truth of those beliefs to make their way to every fiber of one's being. Kierkegaard's emphasis on the paradoxical claim that God became a human—his challenge for Christians to reconsider this belief and allow it to sit within and penetrate their hearts— aims at a generation that *assumes* the incarnation to be true, and will shortly give way to a generation—the liberal theological position—that *hates* or explicitly rejects the claim.

Liberal theology emerged in nineteenth-century Germany with the earnest and understandable goal of helping Christianity respond to changing times. The Scientific Revolution, followed by the Enlightenment, the Romantic period and later Darwinian evolution, all presented challenges to traditional Christian beliefs, and fearing that the only alternatives were a backward-looking dogmatism or giving up the faith altogether, the liberal position tried to steer what it considered to be a middle path. According to theologian Alister McGrath, particular doctrines were either "abandoned, as resting upon outdated or mistaken presuppositions" or "reinterpreted, in a manner more conducive to the spirit of the age."[7] Perhaps *because of* the remarkable discoveries and advancements of the Scientific Revolution and the emboldening intellectual progress of the Enlightenment, confidence in the power of humans to understand and improve the world they inhabited increased to such an extent that the traditional teaching that human nature is fundamentally flawed by sin grew more and more unpopular among European intellectuals and theologians. To put it plainly, Christianity came to be viewed as harsh and over the top, exaggerating what is wrong with humankind. The erosion of the teaching on sin was inextricably tied to doubts concerning the divinity of Christ, which themselves were based significantly on doubts about Scripture. Thomas Jefferson famously constructed his own version of the New Testament, eradicating from it any

[7]Alister McGrath, *Christian Theology: An Introduction*, 4th ed. (Malden, MA: Blackwell, 2007), 82-83.

trace of the supernatural, including references to Jesus' divinity. Minus the traditional doctrine of sin, the received belief in Jesus as the God-human who saves humans from their sin lost its purpose and power. For while it may be true that if humans are supernaturally flawed they need a supernatural savior, it is not so clear how if they *lack* a supernatural flaw they would need a supernatural savior.

Well aware of these changing positions, Kierkegaard challenged the theological establishment but also the layperson who, aware of it or not, had absorbed that theology from the pulpit. One can see both targets in the following admonition: "Admittance [to Christianity] is only through the consciousness of sin; to want to enter by any other road is high treason against Christianity. But sin, that you and I are sinners, has been abolished, or it has been illicitly reduced both in life and in scholarship" (PC 68).

Beyond a strong word to liberal clerics and laypeople, Kierkegaard had a third target in his sights: orthodox theologians of the church past. Kierkegaard himself affirmed Christian orthodoxy, but he rebuked the way of thinking that conceives of ideas such as sin *first* in terms of their doctrinal value. Though sin *is* a doctrine, to think one has exhausted its meaning in speaking this way—that is, to think of sin merely or primarily as a true church teaching—is, ironically, to deny its truth. For the truth of the doctrine of sin—a truth "reduced" in the lives of his contemporaries—can be found not primarily in a detached proposition, say in Romans 3:23, that all have sinned and fallen short of God's glory. Rather its truth is located most properly in the expression of this proposition existentially, or in one's life. When sin is taken this way, then the *making inward* or *appropriation* or *personal absorption* of this doctrine leads to a transformed orientation toward others, oneself and God. Repentance, humility, forgiveness of others and oneself, and clinging desperately to one's savior characterize the Christian whose life existentially expresses the Christian doctrine of sin. Perhaps, Kierkegaard thinks, if Christians were known more by the traits and actions of those deeply aware of their own sin, the Christian witness would be more compelling.

Returning to *Fragments*, Climacus notes how the Socratic picture of sin is one of ignorance, and therefore the remedy is to gain some knowledge. If this is the case, he reasons, then the Socratic picture implies that who the teacher is that conveys the knowledge is not essential for the discovery of that knowledge. The teacher could be Socrates or Plato or Aristotle; it could be a college professor, a TED Talk or Wikipedia. What about the view opposite the Socratic, the view that clearly resembles Christianity? Here the problem is not a lack of knowledge of the good but a lack of the good itself. On this alternative picture sin is not ignorance but instead a function of the free choice of the will that voluntarily heads in the direction opposite of truth. This means that on the alternative/Christian perspective neither a PhD in theology nor a perfect score on a catechism exam gets one closer to religious truth. According to Christianity, the truth is not some bit of knowledge, but rather the truth is a person: "I am the way, *the truth*, and the life," Jesus says (Jn 14:6, emphasis mine). So, Climacus writes, "The object of faith becomes not the *teaching* but the *teacher*" (PF 62). Thus the way out of sin comes not through an education—the gaining of some or another knowledge—but through a relationship with the one who is the truth. While it is correct to say that Jesus educates his follower in word and in deed, following Jesus' teaching does not a Christian make. (Hence Lewis's claim that Jesus is nothing more than a moral teacher is false.) Rather, entering into a relationship to Jesus the Truth is the decisive mark of the Christian.

The liberal theological view ultimately denies that Jesus is the Godhuman, the one who alone saves humans from their sin. This denial, Kierkegaard believes, is rooted in the offense to reason of the paradoxical claim of the incarnation, but also in the offense to the will and its desire for autonomy and self-determination. The alternative to the offensiveness of the incarnation is what Climacus calls the "happy passion" of faith— trusting that God became human and saves us from our sins. As matters of intellectual faith and existential trust, these claims cannot be established by human reason—by logical argument—and therefore Kierkegaard's intention is not *strongly* apologetic but, one might say, *weakly* apologetic. In other words, he aims not to defend Christianity against all forms of secular reasoning, but rather to defend it against slipping orthodoxy. Kierkegaard would rather a "Christian" honestly reflect and openly reject the claims of Christianity than self-deceivingly avoid engaging them and risk living a lie before him- or herself, others and God.

For the Christian today, this twofold challenge remains. First, one must wake up to what others find preposterous about Christianity, as Bono says, reflecting honestly on the radical nature of those claims. This is not a call to doubt or to question beliefs such as the incarnation but rather to avoid the mistake of taking them for granted. And, second, one must allow the transformative implications of those claims to penetrate one's whole life. Ultimately Kierkegaard believes the best proof of Christian truth comes not through argument but through the lives of those transformed by it.

SUFFICIENT SAVIOR

There is little that American culture prizes as much as personal achievement and its tagalong value: self-promotion. Slogans like "do it yourself," "just do it" and "I did it my way" speak to our core belief in personal responsibility, our love of autonomy, and what follows from these things—our need for recognition and credit when we have success. What happens then, when Christians live in such a culture? How do the concerns and cares of achievement or autonomy seep not only into the Christian's vocation and career but into one's understanding of and relation to God? It seems plausible that Christians in such a setting may be tempted to apply the confidence they have in their business acumen, academic prowess or artistic ability to their relationship to God. And on the surface, this might not be so bad: the writer to the Hebrews invites his readers to approach God's throne "with confidence." If through hard work and determination, humans can achieve whatever they set their minds to, as we often tell our children, should Christians be worried that sooner or later they may come to think they can impress God with spiritual skills or commitment to goodness or knowledge of doctrine?

According to author and pastor Timothy Keller, the inclination toward self-determination and autonomy, though especially prevalent in American culture, is in fact the default mode of every human heart. Applied theologically, when this mode of thinking sinks in deep one's orientation to God becomes something like, "I obey; therefore I am accepted."

One's effort and achievements are simply applied to religious tasks—doing good works and obeying the commandments of God. The gospel view, according to Keller, is the reverse: "I am accepted; therefore I obey."[8] Good, obedient behavior is not the *condition for* salvation but the *consequence of* salvation; it comes afterward and reflects a spirit of gratitude. Someone rescued from a burning building is not rescued because she deserves it or because she is really good or really smart. Instead the rescuer freely extends assistance. On being rescued, she will likely show gratitude to the rescuer, though this is not out of obligation as much as it is the natural desire of her heart. If Keller is right that the default tendency of humans and of religious practice specifically is to try to impress God through some variety of holy hard work—what I will loosely call Pelagianism—then this view must be challenged by a biblical conception of Jesus that understands his death on the cross as *sufficient* both for salvation and for holy living.

Pelagianism can take two general forms. The first, more obvious variety, involves behavior. Goodness is the path to God, whether the goodness takes the shape of religious ritual (e.g., sacrifices, church attendance, endless prayer) or moral behavior. The second, perhaps more subtle form involves the mind and gets much more attention from Kierkegaard. Through reasoning well or through believing correct doctrine one makes one's way closer to God. On this view right thinking saves us. Historically the Protestant church has accused the Roman Catholic Church of the first mistake—doing good works to merit God's favor—but the Protestant church has often been guilty of the second.

Kierkegaard challenges the Pelagian tendencies of the human heart and mind in a number of works, including *Philosophical Fragments*, discussed above, and *Practice in Christianity*, another pseudonymous work, which aims to present Christianity in its ideal form. Recall that in *Fragments* the pseudonym Climacus explores how truth is acquired by one who lacks it, and he considers two answers to the question: the Socratic answer and then an alternative position, which clearly resembles the Christian view. To review, to acquire truth on the Christian

---

[8]Tim Keller, "The Meaning of the Gospel," *The Gospel in Action*, accessed July 23, 2015, http://extendingthekingdom.org/?page_id=17.

view one must have a relationship to the teacher *who is* the truth. The Christian view goes a step further, however. Those in untruth not only lack the truth, but they lack the ability to find the truth, or what Climacus calls "the condition." It is like a treasure seeker who not only lacks knowledge of the treasure's location on the beach but cannot even find the beach itself. Put in Christian terms, one needs Jesus, who is "the truth," but what is more—one needs Jesus to see that one needs Jesus. To employ Paul's language, faith—a trusting *relation* to God through Christ—is itself a gift of God. Therefore, Kierkegaard's pseudonym writes, "faith is not an act of will" (PF 62). No amount of "do-it-yourself" exertion will suffice. Clearly this implies that *when* one trusts, believes in or obeys God, these things do not and cannot merit God's favor. "For by grace you have been saved through faith, and this is not your own doing; it is the gift of God—not the result of works, so that no one may boast" (Eph 2:8-9).

Practice in Christianity also emphasizes the initiating action of God in the Christian economy of salvation, though its focus is not on Jesus as "the truth" but on Jesus as "the life" who gives to the broken and dying healing and new life.[9] The scriptural point of departure is Matthew 11:28: "Come to me, all you that are weary and are carrying heavy burdens, and I will give you rest." Kierkegaard imaginatively exegetes the verse by pointing out a dozen or so features of Christ's invitation that distinguish it from traditional healing relationships humans have with their physicians, and a few of these features directly push against the notion that humans somehow play the central role in their own spiritual healing and salvation.

First, in the everyday economy of health and healing the one who shouts "Come here!" is the one in need. The sick seek out the healer; the infirm call on the doctor. Even if a physician makes house calls, the physician must first be contacted. Not so in Christianity, where, by contrast, the one who shouts "Come here!" is actually the healer. "But he who sacrificed himself, sacrifices himself here also, he is himself the one who seeks those who have need of help" (PC 12). To use the language of

---

[9]Kierkegaard also discusses Jesus as the way, thus addressing all three claims of John 14:6. See *For Self-Examination*, 53-70.

Fragments, it is the invitation Jesus offers those in need that provides "the condition" for a relationship with God. Second, ordinarily when a mass invitation is offered—take a television commercial for some new cholesterol-reducing medicine—it turns out that the invitation is far more selective than at first glance. In this example, only those who can afford the new medicine can take advantage of the invitation, even if it claims to be for everyone. Here again one finds the condition for receiving healing to be supplied by the patient, the one in need. It is *my* money that can get me healed. In Christianity, however, "the only one who in truth can help and in truth can help all, consequently the only one who in truth can invite all, he makes no condition whatsoever" (PC 13). The invitation of the earthly healer goes out *not* to all people but to *all who can pay*. But the invitation of Jesus is unconditional—the poor, the ill and injured, the imprisoned, the guilty—all of these are invited. Third, in a similar vein to Climacus's claim above, on the Christian view "the helper is the help" (PC 15). On the ordinary view, the helper's invitation is followed by a "Now leave," after which the needy one is sent out of the healer's presence to find some "analgesic herb" or a "quiet place where he can relax" or a "happier part of the world" (PC 15). The healing process then takes place apart from the healer, who merely sends the ill one on his or her way. The reason for this is practicality: "Ordinarily a physician must divide himself among his many patients" (PC 15). But if the helper is the help and if the help is a constant relationship, then again, there is no work to be done by the one in need, no seeking out the herb, no meditation tricks that will make everything better. The helper's presence is the one thing needed, as Jesus says of Mary's adoration, and it alone is sufficient.

Kierkegaard also critiques an intellectual form of Pelagianism, a view that would count either philosophical cleverness or theological correctness as a way to salvation. Concerning the former, Kierkegaard rejects what we might call the argument from Christendom, a way of reasoning that remains prevalent in regions like the southern United States, where the majority of people identify themselves as Christians. This way of thinking looks at the success of Christianity throughout history or a particular region and chooses to maintain Christian faith at least in part on the basis of this apparent success. In other words, this argument counts as evidence of the truth of Christianity its popularity.[10] However, such argumentation is based not in Christian reflection but in what Kierkegaard calls shrewd calculation and probability, and thus better fits market prognostication or scientific hypothesizing. When one reflects on how often in history large numbers of people have believed obviously false things such as certain claims about the natural world, it becomes readily apparent that truth is not a popularity contest, nor is it a function of the ever-present opinion poll. The argument from Christendom is also unchristian since it is rooted in a kind of probabilistic thinking that says to itself, "What are the odds that this many people could be wrong?" To this Kierkegaard contends, "the truly Christian venturing relinquishes probability" (FSE 98). Applying to Christian faith the sort of thinking that better fits any number of secular arenas, Kierkegaard believes such a strategy reflects "cowardice, the secular mentality, and flabbiness" that wants to be exempted from "dangers and effort and everything that flesh and blood are against" (PC 101). Challenging the notion that the number of professing Christians increases the likelihood that Christian claims are true, Kierkegaard writes, "even if no one had become aware that God had revealed himself in human form in Christ, he still had revealed himself" (BA 118).

So much for shrewd reasoning; what about theological correctness as the way to God? We might grant that human logic is no way to impress God, but certainly our proficiency in theological knowledge is a different story. Right? The problem with this approach is when theology becomes an idol, where one comes to believe that true beliefs conjure God's favor. We have seen above how Kierkegaard rails against the tendency of Christians to exalt doctrine. "When Christianity came into the world . . . it was difficult to become a Christian, and *one did not become preoccupied with understanding Christianity*. Now we have almost reached the parody that to become a Christian is nothing, but it is difficult and a very busy task to understand it" (CUP 371, emphasis mine).

Again, although he affirms Christian doctrine as reflecting God's revealed truth, Kierkegaard believes Christianity is fundamentally an

---

[10]Freshman logic students will recognize the error of this form of argumentation as an appeal to the people (*ad populum*).

existential category rather than an *intellectual* category. In the first place, it concerns the *existence* of God: "Christianity is not a doctrine but the fact . . . that the god has existed as an individual human being" (CUP 326). This implies, as we saw just above, that the object of faith is not a teaching but a person, namely Jesus. If that is the case, then there is no place for pride in one's theology. To conceive of Christianity as an existential category speaks also to the fact that Christians *express* their faith primarily through their lives,[11] "in actuality" as opposed to through the repetition of particular doctrinal claims. This view brings to mind a quotation often attributed to St. Francis: "Preach at all times, if necessary use words." As we saw above, the doctrine of sin is not an end in itself, but it points to how one lives the Christian life—as a humble penitent who seeks forgiveness from God and extends forgiveness to his or her neighbor. The doctrine of the command to love one's neighbor likewise is not an end in itself—something merely to believe or affirm. Rather, love is to be made inward, appropriated, expressed through particular actions and emotions, such as caring for the needy and looking out for others. Jesus did not command us to *think about* loving God and neighbor, but to love God and neighbor. Imagine that the entire world *believes* the command to love to be true statement of human obligation— is the world now more loving? Conversely, imagine that the entire world *expresses* the truth of the command in how people interact with each other; then everything changes. As Paul writes, "If I speak in the tongues of mortals and of angels, but do not have love, I am a noisy gong or a clanging cymbal" (1 Cor 13:1).

To summarize, Kierkegaard believes that when one views Christianity as little more than a collection of truth claims to which one assents, one engages in little more than a clever strategy to justify oneself before God. This strategy is one Scripture seems aware of and abhors. "You believe that God is one; you do well. Even the demons believe—and shudder" (Jas 2:19). The sufficiency of Jesus for salvation and holy living entails that

---

[11]"Primarily" is an important modifier here. Of course Christian truth must be proclaimed, and Kierkegaard explicitly affirms this. "How are they to hear without someone to proclaim him?," Paul writes in Romans 10:14. The point is that the *fundamental* expression of one's Christianity is *a life* that follows Christ, not words that describe how one follows Christ.

no degree or amount of excellence in moral behavior or intelligence—
theological or otherwise—earns the favor of God, but Jesus' redemptive
work alone.

PATTERN

The good news that God's work in Christ is sufficient for salvation
should allay the fears of those who have grown up in a culture of
achievement, people pleasing and pulling oneself up by one's own bootstraps. It should put hearts and minds at rest and strengthen one's trust
in God's love for his creation. And sometimes it does these things.
However, after the gratitude wears off a bit, very often the human tendency is to take this doctrine of grace too far in the other direction and
convert it into a doctrine of license. To Paul's rhetorical question in
Romans 6:1, "Should we continue in sin in order that grace may abound?"
we answer, "Yes, thank you very much." In the following quotation Kierkegaard explains the rationalizations of this "secular mentality" as it
relates to Martin Luther, the great Reformer who was excommunicated
from the Roman Catholic Church for, among other things, preaching
justification by faith alone: "Luther says: It depends on faith alone. . . .
So we take his words, his doctrine—and we are free from all works—
long live Luther! *Wer nicht liebt Weiber, Wein, Gesang / Er wird ein Narr
sein Leben lang* [Who loves not women, wine, and song / He is a fool his
whole life long]" (FSE 16). If God saves me independently of my virtues,
the thinking goes, then he will save me independently of my vices, too.
This is the position I will call grace abuse, a view directly opposite the
Pelagianism described above, yet just as prevalent in today's as in yes-
terday's Christianity. Whereas Pelagianism finds expression in the
human tendency to want to earn God's love, favor and ultimately salvation, grace abuse thinks to itself, if God loves me and promises to
forgive me anyway, I might as well enjoy myself.[12]

Kierkegaard calls grace abuse the cheapening of Christianity, and repeatedly throughout his authorship he talks of how the Christianity of
Christendom has grown, quite literally, worthless. Just as in the world of

---

[12]In my opinion, Christians who reason this way are a greater threat to the witness of the church
than any arguments science, philosophy or psychology can offer.

economics, when the value of some product decreases over time, that product becomes irrelevant and ultimately obsolete.

> The history of Christendom, from generation to generation, became a story of steadily scaling down the price of what it is to be a Christian. At last it came to be such a ridiculously low price that soon it had the opposite effect that people scarcely wanted to have anything to do with Christianity, because through this false leniency it had become so sickly and cloying that it was disgusting. (JFY 189)

Drawn neither from Jesus' call to take up one's cross nor Paul's exhortation to be imitators of God, the requirements of this hollow form of Christianity dissolved into "don't do bad things too much." Cheapened in this way, "Christianity" does not completely disappear, since it provides "a kind of insurance for eternity" (JFY 190). In fact, there may even be "progress in numbers" in spite of or perhaps because of "retrogression in truth" (JFY 208).

Part of why Christianity has been cheapened or scaled down pertains to the universal human tendency to take the path of least resistance. If I am not required to do good works to merit salvation, then why bother doing them at all. There are historical reasons, however, why European Christianity was veering this direction in Kierkegaard's day. Though the story's primary character is Luther, one must first understand what provoked him.

> The Middle Ages conceived of Christianity along the lines of action, life, existence-transformation. This is the merit. It is another matter that some of the actions they hit upon were strange, that it could think that in itself fasting was Christianity, . . . not to mention what we can scarcely mention without smiling—scourging oneself, crawling on one's knees, standing on one leg, etc.—that this was supposed to be true imitation. This was an error. And just as when someone has taken a wrong road and pushes ahead on it, he goes further and further away from the truth, deeper and deeper into error, and it becomes worse and worse—so also here. Something worse than the first error did not fail to appear: they came up with the idea of meritoriousness, thought that they earned merit before God through their good works. And it became worse: they thought they had merit to such a degree through their good works that they thought they

benefited not only the person himself but one could, like a capitalist and bondsman, let others benefit. And it grew worse: it became an out-and-out business: people . . . were put into business as hucksters who sold the good works of others at fixed but cheap prices. (JFY 192)

Thus to speak of cheapened Christianity is not simply to talk in metaphors but refers quite literally to the sale of indulgences, which provoked the ire of Luther and other Reformers. Kierkegaard's history continues,

Then Luther appears. This condition, he declares, is spiritlessness, dreadful spiritlessness; otherwise you who think to earn salvation by good works are bound to perceive that this is the sure road either to *presumptuousness*, consequently to the loss of salvation, or to *despair*, consequently to the loss of salvation. To want to build upon good works—the more you practice them, the stricter you are with yourself, the more you merely develop the anxiety in you, and new anxiety. On this road, if a person is not completely devoid of spirit, on this road he comes only to the very opposite of peace and rest for his soul, to discord and unrest. No, a person is justified solely by faith. (JFY 192-93)

Luther's own anxiety and despair over his sin are well documented. Very clearly his emphasis on justification by faith is a doctrine that offered him great peace and rest. There is no work, no strenuous effort of penance, that can relieve one of sin and the weight of guilt, but solely the work of Christ, which is freely and graciously given through faith.

As we have already seen above, however, it takes little time for humans—now, thanks to Luther, released from penance and anxiety—completely to miss the point of the gospel: that because of Christ's work their lives can express gratitude as living sacrifices in his service. Kierkegaard wraps up his brief history of the road toward cheapened Christianity with an observation about the world in which he lives. "Present-day Christendom, at least that which I am talking about, adheres to Luther; it is another matter whether Luther could acknowledge it, whether the turn that Luther made cannot all too easily become a wrong road as soon as there is no Luther whose life makes the true turn the truth" (JFY 193). Luther might not be able to acknowledge lazy Lutheranism because of his conviction that Christian lives nevertheless produce good works. Instead of earning merit, such works naturally flow from a grateful heart and subsequently serve an evangelistic purpose; they aim "in the direction of witnessing for the truth" (JFY 193).

Aside from his interpretation of history, Kierkegaard articulates the cheapening of grace through a distinction he draws between imitators and admirers. We get a clue about which of the two he takes to be the biblical role in the words of a prayer that precede one of his devotional discourses: "Wake us up, rescue us from this error of wanting to admire or adoringly admire you instead of wanting to follow you and be like you" (PC 233). The prevailing view of Christendom, a view I linked at the beginning of this chapter to all sorts of people today who would never identify themselves as Christians, is to admire Christ. Common sense tells us there is nothing wrong with admiring people—to hold others in high regard, to be in awe at their positive qualities and to be inspired by them. And yet, Kierkegaard clarifies, Jesus did not come to be admired but to get followers, to be imitated. The difference between the admirer and imitator is "an imitator *is* or strives *to be* what he admires, and an admirer keeps himself personally detached" (PC 241). In Christianity's terms, a Christian strives to be like Jesus, while an admirer does not. Kierkegaard makes repeated reference to 1 Peter 2:21: "To this you have been called, because Christ also suffered for you, leaving you an example, so that you should follow in his steps." To follow in Jesus' steps involves drawing near to him as the "pattern,"[13] not keeping a safe distance.

Kierkegaard believes admiration is unfortunately encouraged from the pulpit.[14] Admittedly, preaching is risky because the preacher is expected to model or to imitate the truths expressed in Scripture in his or her own life. In Kierkegaard's day as often in our own, however, this does not occur. "Preaching is abolished," and in its place preachers merely make "observations" (PC 236). Observations may engage Scripture, but they do so in a detached, third-person way. They recount stories, they even speak to spiritual and moral truths of the gospel. But

---

[13]Following some others, I am using the translation "pattern" rather than "prototype," which is the term found in the Hong translations. Both are acceptable, but *prototype* suggests that the thing is to be superseded.

[14]In chapter four we will expand further on the failures of the pulpit and on the call on all Christians to imitate Christ as their expression of witness.

they fail to become first- or second-person; the preacher's words never come "close to either the speaker or listener; the observation very reliably guarantees that it will not become a matter of personal remarks" (PC 236). Kept at a distance, Christian truth can be applauded, Jesus can be admired. Over the course of time parishioners don't know any better since they have not seen by example or been taught that the truths Jesus expresses in his own life are to be expressed in theirs. When admirers of Jesus come across the rare imitator of Jesus, "they refuse to understand that his life should be a demand [on theirs], and if they as much as perceive that he himself understands that it ought to be so, it is already half over with the admiration—they are offended at him" (PC 244). Admirers have different names for imitators—religious fanatic, Jesus freak, fundamentalist and so on.

The true requirement for the follower of Jesus is that one gives one's whole life over; the requirement is "the unconditioned." Just as Jesus' call to the fishermen was to drop their nets and follow him, imitation requires one's life without conditions. Jesus extols the poor widow who, although she gave less money to the temple than others, "put in everything she had, all she had to live on" (Mk 12:44).

Those who do not seek to imitate Jesus and understand him as the pattern for their life do not give up on living good lives altogether, but they believe "the requirement [of Christianity] must be remodeled" (JFY 158). The admirer's strategy involves lessening the requirement to something that suits one better; the admirer converts the "yardstick ... to our size" (JFY 199). This strategy relies on the method of comparison. One looks in the mirror, declares what one sees to be Christian living, and then turns to those whose lives are worse and pats oneself on the back. Kierkegaard offers a humorous anecdote that illuminates the error of this strategy. Out of a class of one hundred students, the thirty with the poorest grades are removed and form a new class. Consequently, the student who previously ranked seventy-first out of one hundred now is number one. Taking pride in being the top student in the second-tier class is like the Christian taking pride in being the best mediocre Christian.

Ultimately, despite the admirer's self-deceived methods of self-justification, "everyone must be measured by the pattern, by the ideal"

(JFY 198). The yardstick for Christian existence is Jesus. If Christians are called to walk in the steps of Christ and be imitators of God, then it seems likely that those who try may fall so far short so as to want to give up. And yet, Kierkegaard reminds his reader, there is no lessening of the requirement despite Christendom's best efforts to do so.

> If Christ had permitted a cheaper edition of being a follower—an admirer who swears by all that is high and holy that he is convinced—then Nicodemus would have been acceptable; then the rich young man who was yet unwilling to give all his goods to the poor and to follow would also have been acceptable . . . ; then that man who merely asked first to bury his deceased father would also have been acceptable; then it would have almost been the case that even King Agrippa, who was "almost persuaded," would have been acceptable. (PC 249)

However close these figures are, Christ refuses to permit a cheaper edition; he refuses admirers.

There is no doubt that Christians who abuse the grace of God through living unchristian lives represent a potential obstacle to those who might have otherwise considered Christianity for themselves, and in chapter four we will explore further what Kierkegaard has to say about Christian witness and the imitation of Christ. There seem to be a variety of reasons Christians tend to abuse God's grace however much they admire Jesus or his followers. Perhaps contemporary American culture has afforded Christians unique strategies to put off imitating Jesus— strategies tied to a dependency on instant gratification and consumerism, where the easiest, quickest and cheapest path is perceived as best. Thankfully, while Jesus is the pattern next to whom all are measured, he is also the savior who forgives our laziness and redeems our failed attempts to follow him.

GENTLE SAVIOR

The requirements of Christian existence, therefore, are very high regardless of human attempts to lower them and regardless of how few actually live up to them. Sadly for us, Jesus' exhortation in the Sermon on the Mount is not to be pretty good because our Father in heaven is pretty good (see Mt 5:48). And the gradual and painful realization that what God asks for is *every* part of *all* of us at *every* moment can be over-whelming and exhausting. Then, just when it seems spiritual progress has been made, Kierkegaard reminds his reader, "no amount of striving exhausts the requirement." In fact, it's more depressing than that: those who strive the furthest are "not one millionth of an inch" closer than the one who never strove at all (JFY 152). This sobering and seemingly unfair claim could cause those earnestly seeking to imitate Christ deep frus-tration, anxiety and hopelessness.

As we saw above, on the experience of feeling "crushed" by the weighty requirement Kierkegaard invites us to turn our eyes on the sufficient savior. "Jesus Christ is not only the pattern but is also the Redeemer, lest the pattern disquiet us to the point of despair" (JFY 159). Kierkegaard supplements this encouraging word by reminding Christians that Jesus the savior not only redeems humans but does so in a radically loving way. In this final section, we will consider Jesus as the gentle savior. Let us turn first to a fairy tale, and second back to Jesus' invitation in Matthew 11:28.

In *Philosophical Fragments* Climacus affirms the uniqueness of Chris-tianity insofar as truth is identified primarily with a personal being, Jesus Christ, rather than a body of knowledge. The second chapter of that book continues the line of reasoning to ask how the relationship comes about between God and human, that is, how humans acquire the truth, and the answer points to God's great love for his beloved. So Climacus decides to tell a love story.

He begins by pointing out that the relationship to humans God ini-tiates is not initiated out of necessity. There is nothing either within God or outside God that requires or forces or necessitates that God create or engage humankind. "But if he moves himself and is not moved by need, what moves him then but love" (PF 24). God *freely* relates to humans, which Climacus takes to be a reflection of divine love. A problem quickly enters in, however. God and humans are far from equals—so far that humans will inevitably fail in any attempt to understand a being as tran-scendent and powerful as God. The resulting predicament is one of "un-happy love"—love that cannot be realized—since the capacities of human understanding are so limited by contrast to God. (A crude analogy may help: many humans love their pet very, very much, yet also feel their pet lacks the capacity fully to understand the depths of their love.) At this point Climacus turns to poetic devices to try to show how God might overcome the great distance between himself and humans to express his love for them. As a work of poetic artistry, the fairy tale veers at moments from a biblical picture of God's relation to humans, although it nevertheless doubles as a kind of argument for why the incarnation had to take place.

"Suppose there was a king who loved a maiden of lowly station in life," the story begins (PF 26). Naturally the king desires the hand of the maiden, but he is overcome "with the sorrow in his heart: whether the girl would be made happy by this, whether she would acquire the bold confidence never to remember what the king only wished to forget—that he was the king and she had been a lowly maiden" (PF 27). What the king seeks is the love of the maiden and yet, as Climacus writes, this is possible only when unequals are made equal. So long as the king remains eminent and the maiden a mere servant, the inequality of their stations in life will disallow genuine love to flourish and the maiden will not feel free to accept his hand.

But how can unequals be made equal? How can the king and maiden unite? First Climacus considers a union "brought about by an ascent" (PF 29). The king could draw the maiden up to himself and exalt her, and the two would be made equal. He could grant her an entire floor in the castle, two dozen servants at her disposal and unlimited spa treatments. However, such a solution would suggest that for the maiden to be loved she must change. And yet the king loves her for who she is—not because he envisions her as a regal queen. This would not promote equality or understanding but would divert attention from his love, since he loves her for who she is, not who she might become. Perhaps rather than drawing her to himself, the king could show up on her doorstep "in all his splendor." "This perhaps would have satisfied the girl, but it could not satisfy the king, for he did not want his own glorification but the girl's" (PF 29). Once more, equality would seem out of reach as the maiden would be dazzled and overcome by the very presence of the king and feel embarrassed in her lowliness, placed in such contrast by his presence. With theological implications bubbling at the surface, Climacus waxes poetic, "Who grasps the contradiction of this sorrow: not to disclose itself is the death of love; to disclose itself is the death of the beloved" (PF 30). While it is possible the maiden would be happy, Climacus notes that the king's love would not be happy since the maiden would cease to be herself, so overcome would she be by his presence.

If unity between the king and maiden cannot come about by ascent—by raising the inferior maiden to the king in all his kingliness—"then it must be attempted by a descent" (PF 30). In other words, the king must come down to the status of the maiden, or at least that is what the reader expects Climacus to say at this point. However, he interrupts the fairy tale to make application to the pressing issue at hand—namely how God loves his creation. "In order for unity to be effected, the god must become like this one . . . in the form of a servant" (PF 31). Though there is consonance with the fairy tale—the maiden is herself a servant—here the pseudonym clearly alludes to a well-known passage in Philippians concerning Jesus' emptying of himself in the incarnation. Speaking of Jesus, Paul writes,

> Who, though he was in the form of God,
>   did not regard equality with God
>   as something to be exploited,
> but emptied himself,
>   taking the form of a slave,
>   being born in human likeness.
> And being found in human form,
>   he humbled himself
>   and became obedient to the point of death—
> even death on a cross. (Phil 2:6-8)

Through the condescension of God in Christ, equality between God and human is made possible. And not only does God come as a human, but God comes as the lowliest kind of human, a servant, so that no other human can feel outside the scope of his loving embrace (PC 239). "Love," Climacus continues, "does not change the beloved but changes itself" (PF 33).

For those weighed down by the demands of Christian existence, Climacus's fairy tale diverts attention away from the anxieties of self-doubt to the picture of a God who is desperate and goes to great pains to communicate his infinite love for his creation, to a God who "so loved the world that he gave his only begotten Son." Putting ourselves in the shoes of the lowly maiden, we can rejoice that our lover cares for us for no other reason than that he cares for us—a most pure form of love. For all of our imperfections we are nevertheless embraced with a divine gentleness that can do nothing other than draw our own love out.

If an extrabiblical poetic reflection on the incarnation of Christ is not a balm for the weary soul, one might turn to the words of Scripture themselves and especially Jesus' invitation in Matthew 11, briefly discussed above: "Come to me, all you that are weary and are carrying heavy burdens, and I will give you rest." Over the course of nearly two dozen pages Kierkegaard ponders the scope of this invitation and reflects specifically on the gentleness of Jesus. We saw above how Jesus invites *all* who are weary, not just those who can pay, not just those who are good, smart or successful in the world. The scope of Jesus' invitation extends not just to all kinds of people but to people with all kinds of unique needs and ailments: "What enormous variety, what almost limitless differences among the invited guests" (PC 16). The text in this section is easily accessible and bears a devotional tone, so I will rely heavily on quotations to convey the sweetness of the invitation.

Kierkegaard first mentions the *lonely*: "Where there is a way so lonely that only one person knows it, one solitary person . . . , so there is only one track, that of the unhappy one who fled down that way with his wretchedness . . . there, too, the invitation finds its way."

Jesus invites the *poor* as well: "Come here, all your poor and wretched, you who must slave in poverty to secure for yourselves—not a carefree but a hard future."

The invitation goes out to the *physically ill and disabled*: "You sick, lame, deaf, blind, crippled, come here!—You who are confined to your beds—yes, you come too, for the invitation has the nerve to invite the bedridden—to come!"

Jesus calls to himself those who experience *emotional suffering*: "You sick at heart, you who know . . . what it means that a physician may be correct in saying that someone has a sound heart but is heartsick."

He invites the *abused*: "All you who have been treated unfairly, wronged, insulted, and mistreated, . . . trampled down in the human mob."

The *suicidal* and *despairing* Jesus invites as well: "Come here, all you sorrowing ones. . . . There certainly is rest in the grave, but to sit beside a grave, or to stand beside a grave, or to visit a grave is still not the same as lying in the grave. . . . In the grave there is rest, but *beside* the grave there is no rest."

Jesus invites those in *relational pain*: "Therefore come here . . . there is rest in the pain of loss—with him who eternally reunites the separated ones more firmly than nature unites parents and children."

Jesus' invitation extends to the *shut-in*, the *outcast*, the *imprisoned*: "Come here . . . you who in the eyes of society are regarded as dead but are not missed, are not lamented."

And, of course, the invitation is also for the *sinner*: "Come here, all you who are lost and gone astray, whatever your error and sin, be it to human eyes more excusable and yet perhaps more terrible, or be it to human eyes more terrible and yet perhaps more excusable, be it disclosed here on earth or be it hidden and yet known in heaven."

Having nearly exhausted the reach of the invitation, Kierkegaard includes one further group lest anyone be left out: "For even if it were possible that utterly pure innocence was to be found somewhere, why should it not also need a Savior who could keep it safe from evil" (PC 16-18).

In exploring the great breadth of Jesus' invitation Kierkegaard thus takes seriously Paul's words to Timothy, that God "desires everyone to be saved" (1 Tim 2:4). Jesus' gentleness is manifest one further way, namely, in *how* he receives those he invites. With the prodigal son's father in mind, Kierkegaard writes, "He makes no difficulty; he does only one thing: he opens his arms" (PC 19). Jesus will not interrogate those who come, nor will he ask them to explain their behavior. He will not rub in the guilt that they may feel. Those who accept the invitation are not shamed, nor are they forced to enumerate their sins. The following passage is among the most moving of all of Kierkegaard's writings:

> And if you are conscious of yourself as a sinner, he will not question you about it, he will not break the bruised reed even more, but will raise you up when you accept him; he will not identify you by contrast, by placing

you apart from himself so that your sin becomes even more terrible; he will grant you a hiding place with himself, and hidden in him he will hide your sins. For he is the friend of sinners. (PC 20)

Lest one feel excluded from the love of God, Kierkegaard hammers home not only the redemptive work of the God-human, Jesus Christ, but the manner of that love, which has gone the greatest lengths to express itself to every human.

In the course of examining a number of erroneous views of Jesus that Christians themselves have long held, the discussion has ended where it should, namely, with attention to the great love and mercy of God in Christ Jesus. Let us turn now to Kierkegaard's description of human existence.

QUESTIONS FOR REFLECTION

1. How do I view Jesus? What difference in my life does my view of Jesus make—not just in terms of beliefs but my emotional life, my motivations, my commitments and my actions?

2. Where does love rank in the list of characteristics or attributes I ascribe to God? How would I think of God if it ranked higher?

3. Am I tempted to doubt or to deny Jesus' divinity, sufficiency, demands or gentleness? What consequences follow if I do?

3

THE HUMAN SELF

Therefore Christ also first and foremost wants to help
every human being to become a self, requires this of him
first and foremost, requires that he, by repenting, become
a self, in order then to draw him to Himself . . . only as
a free being to himself, that is, through a choice.

PRACTICE IN CHRISTIANITY, 160

✝

A SIZABLE NUMBER OF KIERKEGAARD commentators have expressed little interest in and use for Kierkegaard's thought about Jesus Christ and instead have considered his chief insights to be in the area of human existence or psychology, broadly construed. Though, as we will see shortly, his understanding of the human self is theologically rooted, his insights into the human condition are unusually perceptive, and thus it should come as no surprise that those with diverse backgrounds and assumptions should appreciate his thought. The question to which much of his writing provides answers, "What does it mean to be human?" is, after all, among the most fundamental and universal pursuits, dating back as far as Socrates, who devoted his life to this line of inquiry. In Plato's dialogue *Phaedrus*, Socrates explains why he has no time for other intellectual pursuits, including debates about cultural legends, since he still fails to understand what he is himself: "Am I a beast more complicated and savage than Typhon, or am I a tamer, simpler animal with a share in a divine and gentle nature?"[1] For Socrates everything hinges on the question "What or who am I?" If we are *rational animals*, as Aristotle thought, or *not a self* at all, as Buddhism suggests, or thinking things, as Descartes reasoned, or *image-bearers of God*, as the Judeo-Christian tradition teaches, radically different visions of the good life and how to pursue it will follow. Ethical beliefs, to be discussed in chapter five, flow directly from beliefs about what it means to be human. Convictions about how we ought to act proceed from convictions about who we think we are. In the present chapter we turn to Kierkegaard's exploration of selfhood to bring to light our own assumptions and conceptions of this most basic yet far-reaching topic. Kierkegaard was of the opinion that Christianity had the most compelling answer to the question "What does it mean to be human?"

THE CREATED SELF

The starting point for a Christian view of selfhood is the claim that like everything else that exists, human beings are creations of God. Genesis 1:27 and 2:7 tell of God creating the first humans—forming them with earth and breathing into them life—though Christians likewise believe that every subsequent human being *equally* owes his or her existence to God.[2] The church, like the people of Israel before it, has always affirmed that God's creation of humans and the rest of nature occurred *ex nihilo*, out of nothing, which reinforces another doctrine—that God is almighty or omnipotent. God is the sole being for whom all things are possible, and in the creative act God needs no assistance either from other beings or preexisting material from which to work. Kierkegaard affirms God's omnipotence in the creation of all things, but were that the whole story of the Creator's relationship to the creation, he contends, humans would be "nothing"—distanced from their Creator similarly to how plants and animals, mountains and trees in a sense stand removed from God. The notion that humans might enjoy a relationship with God like they enjoy

---

[1]Plato, *Phaedrus* 230a in *Plato: Complete Works*, ed. John M. Cooper, trans. Alexander Nehamas and Paul Woodruff (Indianapolis: Hackett, 1997), 510.

[2]In the New Testament, John 1:3 and Colossians 1:16-17 also speak of God's creation of all things and the role of Jesus Christ in particular.

relationships with one another would not necessarily follow, since acts of omnipotence do not necessitate concern on the part of a creator for the creation.

As we saw in the analogy of the king and maiden, however, it is not power—omnipotence—that explains why or how God creates, redeems and sustains the world, but instead it is love. Unlike the impassible craftsman deity of the classical Greek philosophers who, while powerful, has no personal interaction with or interest in humankind, the God of Abraham, Isaac and Jacob, the God made flesh in Christ Jesus, creates *through* his great power, but creates *from* or *out of* deep love, and thereby establishes in the creative act a relationship with them.[3]

Thus, on Kierkegaard's view, the human self is immediately *outwardly relational*. It is a being that comes into existence already in relationship with another being, God, just as a newborn is already in relationship with his or her parents. Just as the newborn does not have a say in having two particular parents or any parents at all, so too are all humans related to God independent of their choosing.[4] And just as being born into a human family comes with certain expectations, so too are there expectations on the lives of humans by virtue of being creations of God. Significantly, though, just as a relation to God is made possible by God's love and not by his power, Kierkegaard believes God's expectations for humans are likewise rooted in his love and not in his power: "Omnipotence does not require anything [of humans]; it never occurs to omnipotence that a human being is anything other than nothing. . . . But the loving God, who in incomprehensible love made you something for him, lovingly requires something of you" (CD 128). What could this mean? What hinges on expectations coming from divine love rather than divine power? Imagine again an analogy to human parenting. The expectations I have for my daughter to behave kindly or to try new food or to discern

---

[3]The twentieth-century French philosopher Simone Weil defines divine power in light of divine love, sharing the conviction with Kierkegaard that creation is fundamentally an expression not of the former but of the latter: "On God's part creation is not an act of self-expansion but of restraint and renunciation" (*Waiting for God* [New York: Harper Perennial, 2009], 89).

[4]There might be another important analogy here. Just as a baby who does not yet have a grasp on language and concepts is thus not significantly conscious of his or her parents *as* his or her parents, so too do humans created by God often have no significant consciousness of God as their heavenly Father.

her vocation come not from my ability as her father to command her thus (power), but instead from my hopeful desire to see her become a person of character, to see her reach her richest potential and become the best self she can become (love). I wish these things for her and subsequently command her thus because I love her, not because I wish to express my parental power. Kierkegaard's point here seems indirectly confirmed when we consider our natural censure of parents who "discipline" their children with an arbitrary iron fist as if on a power trip, as if they were tyrants who act not out of concern for the good of their children but out of the sheer exercise of their will.

A few things follow from Kierkegaard's analysis of power and love. First, as creations of a loving God, humans are not autonomous beings, subject ultimately to themselves. While Christians without much difficulty confess this truth, the challenge comes in feeling its weight in the face of the gale force of contrary opinion in Western culture. Especially since the Enlightenment and the development of classical liberal political thought, and all the way through the existentialism of the twentieth century and postmodernism today, the idea that humans are *not* finally in charge of themselves is one of the most scandalous claims of Christianity. At every turn the message that each of us is our own ultimate authority is reinforced. Second, those who are offended or disgusted by the ostensibly infantilizing idea of a despotic God commanding his little creations may be operating with a faulty theology of the commander, a sort of straw man position. If the requirements God makes on human lives proceed fundamentally from love, and not from force, just as the requirements of the ideal loving parent proceed fundamentally from love, and not from force, then critiques of faith relying on certain theological caricatures miss their target.

But there is a third implication. According to Kierkegaard, one of the greatest signs of God's love for humankind is the gift of freedom they possess in relation to him. In a number of devotional writings Kierkegaard gleans lessons from Jesus' discussion of the lilies and birds in the Sermon on the Mount (Mt 6:25-34). In *Christian Discourses* these lessons concern a variety of worries or "cares" that consume us, including the difficulties that accompany poverty and abundance, lowly and lofty social status, and even the desire to move up the social ranks. There are limits to the lessons one can learn from the lilies and birds, however, and the point of divergence pertains specifically to freedom. With Matthew 6:24 in mind,[5] Kierkegaard writes,

> The poor bird of the air and the humble lily of the field do not serve two masters. Even though the lily does not serve God, it still serves only to God's honor. . . . The bird does not serve two masters. Even though it does not serve God, it exists only to God's honor, sings to his praise, does not demand at all to be anything itself. So it is with everything in nature; that is its perfection. But that is also its imperfection, because there is therefore no freedom. The lily standing out there in the open field and the free bird of the air are nevertheless bound in necessity and have no choice. (UDVS 205)

Though artists, poets and musicians have not infrequently used birds to represent freedom, spiritually speaking they are like all other animals (and plants) in their lack of free will. Humans, by contrast, are not bound in necessity but instead possess the capacity to choose, a capacity Kierkegaard calls our "glorious treasure . . . not intended to be buried and concealed" (UDVS 206). This treasure is an expression of God's love because it reflects *how* he wishes to engage in a relationship with humans—freely—and because it assumes a renunciation of his power, just as the king who takes the form of a lowly servant to become equal to the lowly maiden expresses his love for her. Commenting on the gift of human freedom, Kierkegaard writes,

> Do you know of any more overwhelming and humbling expression for God's condescension and extravagance towards us human beings than that he places himself, so to say, on the same level of choice with the world, just so that we may be able to choose; that God, if language dare speak thus, woos humankind—that he, the eternally strong one, woos sapless humanity? (UDVS 206)[6]

Having placed himself on the level of the world for humans to choose between, God nevertheless stipulates that a choice must be made, human

---

[5]"No one can serve two masters. Either you will hate the one and love the other, or you will be devoted to the one and despise the other. You cannot serve both God and money."

[6]I have chosen Charles Moore's translation here; *Provocations: Spiritual Writings of Kierkegaard* (Walden, NY: Plough, 2002), 9-10.

freedom must be exercised. There is no neutral position, no way to avoid the choice of God or the world. In other words, a failure to choose God is no different from choosing against God. "If God has lowered himself to being that which *can be chosen*, then a person indeed *must* choose— God is not mocked" (UDVS 207). For Kierkegaard this caveat buttresses two important theological convictions. God can be loved freely through a choice. And yet, however one chooses—even if one thinks one can abstain—God's power is honored because a choice is nevertheless made.

This scriptural picture of choosing God or the world seems black and white, all or nothing, and maybe in the end that is the way things are. Perhaps a close analysis of every moment of our lives would reveal this to be the case. And yet most of us are at least occasionally aware of our motivational duplicity—our sometimes unconscious, sometimes conscious desire to have our cake and eat it too when it comes to God. We claim to do something for God or convince ourselves something is the right thing to do, all the while serving the unchecked and unholy desires of our hearts, desires that our reputation be elevated or our personal agenda be met. If one has confronted this inner duplicity, one can testify that exercising freedom to choose God over the world is not something one can master this side of heaven. It is a difficult and seemingly endless task, one that speaks to how humans are, in Kierkegaard's language, always in the process of *becoming*. Whereas a bird "is what it is," a human being through freedom is a dynamic creature capable of progressing or regressing, of stagnating or evolving.

These observations about becoming offer a pair of initial insights for Christian selfhood. First, as odd as it sounds, Christians *become* Christians. That is, to be a Christian means to choose to be a Christian (to choose God) at every moment. As free creatures, Christians cannot flip on a spiritual cruise-control switch any more than they can escape to a world free of temptation. Rather, one always has the opportunity to choose the creation over the Creator, as Paul writes in Romans 1:25 and St. Augustine echoes in his *Confessions*. The Christian has not yet arrived. Second, this means that one cannot wear the label "Christian" as a badge of perfection or superiority. If Christians are becoming Christians, then part of the Christian witness involves testifying to God's steadfast love *in the midst* of one's ups and downs, one's choices for and against God, one's sinfulness. It follows then that Christians should be known for their moral and spiritual humility; the term *Christian* should connote to others a repentant and forgiving spirit. Christian lives are public stories for others to read and discover the work of God. They are not marketing opportunities to show how great one is or how easy things get when you sign on the dotted line, how smart or successful those who are saved are or become.

Given his emphasis on human freedom it is no wonder why some champion Kierkegaard as the father of existentialism, a philosophy that prizes choice as the central feature of human existence and emphasizes the importance of defining oneself. For Kierkegaard, however, freedom and choice are not radical, as they are for some existentialists, and this can be seen in two ways. First, if humans are created beings, then freedom itself is a condition of being unfree with regard to one's very existence. An individual's existence is not an absurd, random fact of the universe. Rather, a loving God creates us, and this comes with expectations that constrain our freedom. Second, we often use our freedom in ways that lead, oddly enough, to a loss of that very freedom. Imagine a child is given five dollars and would like to purchase both a doll and a book but can only afford one. She freely chooses the doll and in so doing becomes unfree with regard to her ability to acquire the book. In a stronger sense, human moral freedom, to be discussed at length below, allows one to choose sinful actions, the consequences of which often if not always result in spiritual unfreedom or spiritual bondage.

Christian freedom is real, though it is not radical, and when it operates properly and ideally, it operates in conjunction with God's action, so that humans are joyful colaborers or co-agents with God. To illustrate this conditioned form of freedom Kierkegaard tells the story of Ludwig, a little boy whose mother regularly takes him on stroller rides. One day she thinks of a new idea that will delight little Ludwig; she invites him to push his own stroller. Ludwig cannot push the stroller all by himself, and in reality it is his mother standing above him who is doing the work. Ludwig thus enjoys a measure of freedom within certain constraints of his own ability, though he is sustained in his work by his mother. Importantly, because assisting her son comes from love and not from an exertion of power, the mother finds that the activity of freely pushing the stroller fulfills the child: "His face is shining with happiness" (JFY 185). Later when Ludwig grows up and reflects on the experience, he does not feel deceived but "has another joy" at the expression of love by his mother, that she would allow him a measure of self-determination (JFY 186). Through this anecdote Kierkegaard suggests that humans are most free when they recognize the loving authority of God, who wills their good and constrains their freedom for the sake of their good. The conventional wisdom of the post-Enlightenment world suggests the opposite—that with God and God's will and commands comes a yoke that leads to bondage, to inauthenticity, and to a loss of genuine selfhood. Instead the opposite is true; through his loving authority God's will is that humans should have their own will and in its proper execution become the self they were created to be.

THE DEEP SELF: ANXIETY AND FREEDOM

We have seen how humans are *outwardly relational* beings insofar as they are creations of a loving God (not to mention offspring of human parents). Humans are also *inwardly relational* in that the self is a multi-layered and complex entity. That this is the case is immediately apparent when we contemplate our own rationality. Like dogs and cats, humans have the capacity to think, but unlike dogs and cats (or at least my dogs and cats) human rationality allows one to think about thinking, to reflect on oneself and then reflect on that reflection, to introspect, even to disagree with ourselves. Most of us have had experiences in which a desire conflicts with a duty, or one feels remorse for some action even though it felt good at the time. The apostle Paul testifies to the complex stratification of his own heart: "I do not understand my own actions. For I do not do what I want, but I do the very thing I hate" (Rom 7:15). St. Augustine, too, recounts how while hearing the testimony of a friend, God sought to bring unity to his conflicted soul: "But You, Lord, while he was speaking, turned me back towards myself, taking me from behind my own back where I had put myself all the time that I preferred not to see myself."[7] These dizzying scenarios of inner conflict illustrate that we have deeper, multilayered selves, but also that because of this we experience difficulties unknown to the rest of creation, dogs and cats included.

It is this multilayered dimension of the human self that Kierkegaard views as central to the notion that humans are spiritual beings. "A human being is spirit. But what is spirit? Spirit is the self. But what is the self? The self is a relation that relates itself to itself or is the relation's relating itself to itself in the relation; the self is not the relation but is the relation's relating itself to itself" (SUD 13). Clearly, from this definition self-reflection and introspection are distinguishing marks of human personhood. But the self's inward relationality is more than these things, since the self is inwardly relational whether or not one is aware of it—whether one regularly self-reflects or introspects. Kierkegaard further specifies the self's relational makeup through a list of several paired concepts. They include the following: the *eternal* and *temporal*, the *infinite* and *finite*, *freedom* and *necessity*, and the *psychical* and *physical*. Each human is a combination of these contrasting features, which speaks all the more to how unique humans are by comparison with the rest of creation. On paper these pairings evoke a kind of harmony or symmetry, but in reality they are often in tension in human lives, and sometimes one side of the pairing completely overrides the other. As we will explore below, Kierkegaard associates the misrelation within these pairings with human sinfulness and despair, which, if true, is suggestive of the numerous varieties human sin can take and corroborates Jesus' words "the gate is wide and the road is easy that leads to destruction" (Mt 7:13).

The complicated interactions and misrelations within the self that are manifest in the push and pull of these pairings are not resolved simply by moving toward the *expansive pole*, by favoring infinitude, eternity, freedom or the psychical. After all, humans are concrete, finite creatures who live in time and who constantly face constraints on their freedom. Neither, however, does inner peace come through focusing attention and effort on the *limiting pole*, embracing solely one's finitude, temporality, physicality and the necessity that seems to bind one. So how does one

---

[7] Augustine, *Confessions*, trans. F. J. Sheed, ed. Michael P. Foley (Indianapolis: Hackett, 2006), 152.

find balance in all of this? First, let us note that Kierkegaard thinks that to have a self with *all* of these incongruous elements is "the greatest concession," that the freedom humans possess can serve the end of bringing these elements into harmony (SUD 21). Having said this, Kierkegaard believes that this process will not succeed if left to humans alone, given the obvious limits on their freedom and ability and the tendency, described above, to use freedom in self-destructive ways. As in Matthew 11, Kierkegaard thinks the solution to the disharmony within the self is to accept Christ's invitation to rest in him. Only through finding one's identity, meaning, story, motivation, and marching orders in one's loving Creator can despair be overcome.

With this basic structure of the self in mind, let us turn to the more familiar idea of sin, a concept fundamental to Kierkegaard's psychological thought, and one he finds helpful in describing the self's failure to rest transparently in God. Kierkegaard defines sin in the following way: "*before God, or with the conception of God, in despair not to will to be oneself, or in despair to will to be oneself*" (SUD 77, emphasis original). The first thing to note about this definition is that sin is a *theological* position; it is a statement primarily about one's relation to God rather than an assessment of one's goodness or badness.[8] Following from this, second, sin is not to be identified with bad actions, such as those prohibited in the Ten Commandments. Rather, it is a *condition* of the self, and specifically the self's relationship to God, that gives rise to those particular bad actions we call sins. Third, the definition articulates that the root of this condition is the desire for self-rule, for autonomy (which can be traced back to the story of Adam, Eve and the serpent). The consequence of understanding sin not as reducible to particular actions but instead as a condition or way of relating to God is that it demonstrates how even "good people," those who do righteous or holy or just things, nevertheless suffer from the sin-condition insofar as they construe their righteousness as a product of their and only their own efforts of self-

---

[8]In light of this we might critique G. K. Chesterton's famous claim that original sin is empirically verifiable and the only Christian doctrine that can be proved. Chesterton is undoubtedly correct that the claim that all people do rotten things is easy to confirm through observation, but what cannot be observed is that such actions offend against God, however true this may be.

actualization. Fourth, what makes sin particularly pernicious is its self-destructiveness; the one who sins works *against* his or her own good, moves away from his or her true self.

Kierkegaard understands sin primarily as a theological, not psychological concept, though he believes that psychology can study what comes before sin (sin's antecedents) as well as the consequences of sin. Before proceeding further, however, let us pause to acknowledge what Kierkegaard is doing when he considers sin in just this way, because there are broader implications for Christian learning and scholarship. In exploring a theological concept with the insight of a discipline other than theology (or a text other than the Bible), Kierkegaard seems to take up the Augustinian point of view that all truth belongs to God no matter where one finds it. Just because one approaches some topic from a nontheological or even non-Christian position does not mean such a position is inappropriate, wrongheaded or incapable of shedding light on that concept. Second, and related, by approaching a theological doctrine from the nontheological perspective of psychology Kierkegaard potentially reinvigorates the Christian's understanding of an important theological concept that has grown all too familiar and stale, opening Christians up to new ways of thinking about concepts important to their faith.

The Christian biologist and distinguished professor Jeffrey Schloss provides a helpful example of this. He tells the story of a scientific study on voles, small rodents that resemble mice, that he thinks might have fruitful implications—believe it or not—for how pastors counsel married couples.[9] Scientists were curious why one species of vole, the meadow vole, was promiscuous (mated with multiple partners) while another species, the prairie vole, was monogamous. They found that the monogamous vole had more oxytocin, a bonding hormone present in mammals that increases the likelihood that a mating pair stays together. A single gene accounts for this trait, and the scientist inserted the gene into a meadow vole. As a result the meadow vole became monogamous. Interestingly, humans possess this gene, which should confirm for Christians God's intention that marriage partners be faithful to one another.

---

[9]Dr. Schloss made these remarks at a Science for Ministry seminar, "Evolution in Cosmology, Biology, and Theology," at Princeton Theological Seminary in September 2010.

But Schloss commented further that what this genetic insight suggests is that if we suppose there could be genetic attachment disorders in humans, that is, disorders in which one's oxytocin levels are abnormal, then clearly some humans will have a more challenging time bonding to a spouse in the ways we expect of faithful partners. In turn, this unlikely insight from biology might inform how pastors, therapists and fellow Christians love their parishioners, clients and neighbors and treat those who struggle with faithfulness. Returning to our present topic, Kierkegaard similarly believes that exploring sin not through the hard sciences but through a psychological lens may help us to understand and deal with our sin in a more meaningful way.

For Kierkegaard anxiety precedes sin, though by anxiety he does not mean what Freud or contemporary behavioral therapists mean. Anxiety is not a result of repressed sexuality or a signal of a threat to the personality, nor is it simply a conditioned response to an external stimulus. Importantly, anxiety is not inherently pathological but rather is a universally human phenomenon crucial for selfhood. The reason for this is that anxiety closely accompanies freedom. Kierkegaard defines anxiety as "*a sympathetic antipathy* and *an antipathetic sympathy*" (CA 42, emphasis original). It occurs when one is attracted to and repulsed by the same thing. When someone's desires are unambiguously in one direction, one's freedom to choose one way over another does not produce anxiety. For example, when a student both wants to earn an A on an exam and is committed to studying for the exam, anxiety as Kierkegaard understands it is not produced. This holds true even if the student is worried about passing the exam. We might say the choice to study was natural, or the two desires—to earn an A and to study—were consistent with each other, and thus this person might have acted with little conscious awareness that the actions were free, that choice was involved. However, when one's desires are in conflict with each other, then the result is anxiety. Suppose a student wants to earn an A but doesn't want to do the work for an A. She is attracted and repulsed by the same thing: a good grade. She is attracted by the intrinsic reward or prestige of an A but repulsed by the challenge and cost of earning it herself; she may be repulsed but also attracted to the idea of cheating in order to secure the A.

This simultaneous desire for and aversion toward getting the A produces anxiety because it forces her in freedom finally to make a choice, to take a course of action, and of course there are pros and cons on each side. Anxiety conceived in this way might be understood as a *revelatory emotion* insofar as an anxiety-laden scenario like this discloses or reveals the power and ability one has to choose. Suppose our student is young and to this point in her education things have always come easy to her, but this is the first time she's been faced with a difficult A. The anxiety of the attraction/repulsion not only forces her to choose, but in so doing it makes her aware of the significant freedom she has. It *reveals* that not only can she study or not study, but she can cheat or simply not take the exam at all. Nothing we've said thus far suggests the student will sin or do something immoral, but it takes little imagination to see how sin can easily follow this experience of anxiety. Thus anxiety is not the same as sin and does not entail sin, but it can precede sin.[10]

If anxiety, like freedom, is a universal human trait, but sin does not necessarily result from anxiety, does Kierkegaard deny the doctrine of original sin? Is it *not* the case that all *necessarily* sin and fall short of the glory of God (Rom 3:23)? The short answer is no. Kierkegaard affirms the sinful nature of humans (the Danish *Arvesynd* literally means inherited sin) but is emphatic that one cannot blame Adam and Eve for one's own sin. Just as Adam sinned freely, so too does each individual. "*Sin came into the world by a sin*" (CA 32, emphasis original). Freedom understood in part through the experience of anxiety enables the possibility of sin, but as to why sin was chosen, there is no external answer to be found, ultimately no blame to place on others. One cannot blame the devil or another human: "How sin came into the world, each man understands solely by himself" (CA 51).

But we might press the point further. How can one affirm both that (a) a sinful nature is passed down one human to another and (b) when a human sins there is no one else to blame? The worry here is that it would

---

[10]Kierkegaard's view of anxiety thus seems compatible with the moral psychology of James 1:14-15: "But one is tempted by one's own desire, being lured and enticed by it; then, when that desire has conceived, it gives birth to sin, and that sin, when it is fully grown, gives birth to death."

seem unfair if humans were set up to fail, if because of Adam's sin the rest of us had no choice but to sin as well. Kierkegaard's answer to this draws on a careful distinction between *sin* and *sinfulness*. Humans have inherited *sinfulness*, which refers both to the tendency to sin and the multiplicity of ways to sin, from Adam. And thanks to him and other sinful predecessors, the number of ways humans can sin has increased in number. The growth of the internet and the unfettered access to pornography, online gambling and increased opportunities to slander and gossip via social media illustrate this in our own day—there are literally more ways to sin than there used to be. So, humans inherit sinfulness, the propensity to sin, and the ways to sin have increased. Sinfulness, however, is not itself sin, and we do not inherit sin from Adam. Having tendencies to sin no more makes one guilty of sin than having musical ability makes one a great musician. There is no direct transition from a capacity to an action, from sinfulness to a sin. Thus, although we have inherited a tendency, *sinfulness*, we only *sin* through our own free action. We only sin when we choose to sin.

Anxiety is not just the antecedent of sin but the consequence of sin as well. That is, after someone sins, a new kind of anxiety results. The reason is that after sinning the individual experiences guilt over the sin.[11] While Kierkegaard believes guilt can be a genuine and appropriate response, it can also become a new source of anxiety if it is not brought before God. In fact, one may approach one's guilt and embrace it as one last shred of something one has control over; one can use guilt to serve the purposes of autonomy and self-assertion. This could happen through a refusal to seek or to accept forgiveness for a wrongdoing. It could also be seen when one takes pride over one's fallen state. Though guilt can be a teacher that prods one to seek God, guilt can serve the opposite purpose of keeping God at a distance. Returning to our scenario of the student faced with the exam, let us suppose the student decides to cheat. On cheating she then feels bad about her actions and wishes to confess her guilt. Yet

---

[11]Guilt could mean two things here. First, there is the mood or feeling of having done something wrong. Second, there is a legal status, which we mean when we say someone is found "guilty." That these senses are not identical is clear when we consider that a criminal found guilty of a crime can nevertheless not feel guilty, and someone found not guilty of a crime *can* feel guilty. In this context we are speaking of the first sense of guilt—the mood or feeling.

simultaneously she does not wish to confess her guilt since that would be just that—a confession, an admission of wrongdoing. Anxiety preceded her sin, but anxiety seems to result from it as well.

THE DEEP SELF: DESPAIR AND SIN

Anxiety is therefore closely tied to sin, but it is not identical to sin. Despair, on the other hand, Kierkegaard *identifies* with sin. This may strike us as odd for at least two reasons. First, despair seems like an emotional state—it literally means the loss or absence of hope—and yet most of us don't think of sin as an emotional state. Second, given the emotional connotation, we tend to tie despair to depression, and often we do not think of those who are depressed as somehow culpable before God for their depression. As we will see, Kierkegaard's view of despair is something rather different.

First, despair is a condition or state of the self, and while he believes despair may rise to the surface and materialize in the form of some mood, that is by no means necessary, and neither does he think such despair is common. This means that despair like we usually think of it could be a subset of Kierkegaard's broader category of despair, but it would by no means exhaust that category. Second, we tend to think of despair as necessarily having an object—as despair *over* lost love or despair *over* bad news. Kierkegaard claims that ultimately despair's object is always the self, and therefore the despairing moods we sometimes experience really reflect a subterranean problem of selfhood. Though there seems to be a resemblance, despair in Kierkegaard's sense cannot be identified with the modern psychological category of depression. Depression is a complex state, with many possible types of causes, but the general view of depression seems to be that it is a pathological medical condition, at least sometimes caused by physiological factors in the brain. For Kierkegaard, despair, since it is identical to sin, is universal among humans, something that is only overcome through faith in God, and even then, perhaps only partially for many people. It is not a disease caused by physical factors or even a state that is induced by some external problem, but a spiritual state grounded in the choices of the self. Of course despair in this sense can overlap with cases of depression, but it cannot simply be identified with depression. Many people psychologists would consider in good mental health are in despair according to Kierkegaard.

If despair is identical to sin, then by definition despair is basically a failure to be oneself or to be a self at all. Specifically, despair, like sin, pertains to *not* choosing (or willing) to be the self God created one to be, and if every human self is a complex balance of the sets of paired concepts noted above, then one way of gaining clarity about despair is through a *symptomatic analysis* that considers the ways these relational pairings are manifest properly or improperly in the personality, that is, what happens when the finite or infinite parts of the self, for example, are not balanced. Let us look at a few of different forms despair can take.

Infinitude's despair. Despair of *infinitude* occurs when one lacks finitude. Put plainly, this person fails to recognize the limits of existence. To lack finitude is to live in a fantasy realm where one's imagination knows no bounds and is in charge of the projects and cares of one's life. When one gives one's life over to an alternate reality that bears little resemblance to the real world with all of its actual constraints, this individual drifts "away from himself and thereby prevents him from coming back to himself" (SUD 31). To lack finitude is to forget or ignore the parameters of human life, whether they concern what is possible in terms of life goals or what is permissible in terms of behavior. The main character of Kierkegaard's pseudonymous "The Diary of a Seducer" (EO), Johannes the seducer, seems to suffer with this kind of despair. Johannes seeks the affections of a young woman, Cordelia, and has made a sort of game over winning her over. His seduction goes beyond the usual attempt of convincing someone to engage in sexual intercourse. Johannes aims to convince Cordelia that *she* is seeking him. His attempt to alter her reality and bring it in line with his own fantasy is a manifestation of his skewed vision of the world and his apparent ignorance or refusal to accept the finite limitations that bear on his actual existence. One of the remarkable features of the diary is that as it progresses, it grows more and more difficult for the reader to tell what is going on in the actual narrative and what is going on in Johannes's imagination. This intentional ambiguity on Kierkegaard's part brilliantly captures a kind of despair that "prevents him from coming back to himself." Johannes has no sense of himself because he lives in a make-believe realm. Ironically the seducer is the victim of his own seduction.

Finitude's despair. One may despair in the opposite direction by lacking *infinitude*. Whereas Johannes the seducer's blurred vision could not see finite reality at all, the one who despairs the opposite way has no sense of anything beyond the finite realm—beyond what one can see or touch or measure or purchase. More common than its counterpart, this form of despair maintains a secular mentality that "is nothing more or less than the attribution of infinite worth to the indifferent," and is characteristic of those who "mortgage themselves to the world" (SUD 33, 35). The fundamental mistake of this form of despair is that infinite weight or importance or priority is knowingly or unknowingly projected onto finite objects of interest and concern (read: anything but God). I will do *anything* to get that ___ (fill in the blank with job, man/woman, boat, home, etc.). Imagination concerning things beyond the here and now is all but absent, so that one's conception of the goods of human existence is exhausted by wealth or power or social status or family (or video games, college sports, hobbies, etc.). Clearly this form of despair seems strongly compatible with atheistic worldviews that value only those things that matter this side of the grave. However, theists too can despair this way if the God they believe in is little more than a divine Santa Claus whose purpose is to dispense more finite goods. Theists can also despair this way if they love God's creation more than God.

Possibility's despair. There is also the despair of *possibility*, freedom's despair, which lacks the limiting feature of necessity. What does this mean? We have established that freedom is essential to human existence and of chief importance for Kierkegaard, but here we see further why he believes that a radical freedom in which one fully defines oneself and one's own purpose runs aground. Kierkegaard writes, "What is missing is essentially the power to obey, to submit to the necessity in one's life, to what may be called one's limitations" (SUD 36). This form of despair is thus defiant in its refusal to admit any imposition on its freedom, including the will or the commands of a loving God. According to Alvin Plantinga it is this defiance that lies behind much atheism, and not reasoned arguments. Though one might claim there is insufficient evidence to believe in God, Plantinga thinks that the real offense is not against one's reason but against the will.[12] In a different way despair of possibility can also be observed in the lives of those we sometimes pejoratively call dreamers, who—perhaps suffering also from the despair of infinitude— groundlessly believe they can do whatever they want or whatever they put their mind to. Dreamers make exciting plans and passionately recruit others to share in their enthusiasm, but rarely are the plans successfully executed if they are even begun. This dreamy mentality may be fostered in our culture's achievement worship as we encourage our children that they can do anything they want if they work hard enough. This advice might serve as useful motivation but it falls short of wisdom, since it often comes without the caveat of limitations (and since it is false). There is little more pathetic than grown adults who frequently describe grandiose visions for their future that will never materialize. Here too we can see that this person lacks awareness of necessity, of the way things actually operate in a world full of constraints and limitations that exist independent of our choosing and willing.

Necessity's despair. Conversely, one might despair of *necessity*, might lack the hope that possibility affords free human selves. More than the other forms of despair, Kierkegaard correlates this position to a unique religious failing—namely, to believe that for God all things are possible. Above we defined God's omnipotence as the doctrine that for God all things are possible, and while Christians affirm this without much trouble or confusion, it can be difficult to rest in its truth when one confronts the stubborn realities of life. While every human experiences some moments of hopelessness, the case of the addict lucidly illustrates this form of despair. Addicts not only struggle with the object of their addiction and its damaging effects on their body and mind, but also their struggle can be compounded by a hopelessness that things will never change, which can in turn reinforce the addiction. Such a person might be able to contrive the mental picture of a future without the addiction, but nevertheless trusting that this is a

---

[12]Plantinga makes this point in an interview by Gary Gutting on a *New York Times* blog about the irrationality of atheism, "Is Atheism Irrational?," *The Stone* (blog), February 9, 2014, http://opinionator.blogs.nytimes.com/2014/02/09/is-atheism-irrational.

real and not simply an *imagined* possibility is another thing altogether. Whether the hopelessness pertains to our own case or to someone else, the person who despairs of necessity cannot rest in God, for whom all things are possible, and instead feels a victim of fate, circumstances, genes or past decisions.

While those who despair in these and other ways could have a variety of distinct personality traits, the common thread of each form of despair is the self's desire—conscious or not—to determine who it will become and how if at all it will relate to God. Whether in weakness or in strength, through passivity or defiance, every effort *not* to be the self God created one to become is a form of despair and therefore sin. When the pairings are out of sync the self has freedom to remedy the imbalance to resemble better the ideal self as God created it, though ultimately God's help is required for despair and sin to be overcome. For in the end no amount of do-it-yourself exercises will suffice. And this seems to follow if in fact the core of despair and sin is self-definition and self-rule.

THE DEVELOPING SELF

Having described several of the ways one can willfully dodge genuine selfhood, let us turn to Kierkegaard's understanding of human development, which offers a different picture of how a fragmented self can properly move toward wholeness and a transparent, restful relation with God. Over the course of several books Kierkegaard delineates three well-known stages of existence: the aesthetic, ethical and religious. He elucidates these stages not theoretically, as though he were writing for an audience of scholars or clinical therapists, but poetically, through stories and through perspectives of various characters and pseudonyms that belong to the stages and thus speak from particular, stage-specific perspectives. There are many reasons Kierkegaard employs these methods, but one is undoubtedly to serve the missionary aim of pointing out to Christians how their own lifestyles reflect something other than Christianity. Kierkegaard believes that communicating moral and religious ideas indirectly through narrative is more able to draw readers in and evoke a genuine, personal response than direct approaches like sermons, lectures or treatises.

The term *stage* implies that one proceeds in order from the first to the last and that they together follow a natural progression, and so a human life properly unfolds in the direction of the religious. In this sense the stages of existence present a kind of ideal picture of how human selfhood can be attained, in which a relation to God matches up with human flourishing or the attainment of genuine selfhood. Yet Kierkegaard also refers to these as *spheres* of existence, modes of living, which does *not* suggest a natural progression. The reason for this can be found precisely in the notion of human freedom. If one is genuinely free, then one may choose not to leave one sphere for another; one may well choose to remain an aesthete, for example.

Aesthetic derives from the Greek *aesthesia*, which means sensation, and while Kierkegaard's use of aesthetic has other meanings as well, it is fair to say that those in the aesthetic sphere are generally driven by sensation, by desire and often (though not always) by the moment at hand. Aesthetic existence is the default position of human life; it is the sphere of the young child. It is natural for children to be motivated by immediate desires, by the present moment and by the senses, and thus to some extent the child's aesthetic existence might be viewed as innocent. After all, it seems natural and suitable to the survival of a newborn to have *only* immediate concerns to have its desires for food, warmth and safety fulfilled. It is clear, however, that some people remain in the aesthetic sphere long after childhood ends.

Aesthetic existence includes a range of possibilities, from those whose lives are characterized by "pure immediacy" (e.g., a very young child) to those whose lives are characterized by a heightened degree of reflection, like Johannes the seducer. To call an aesthete immediate speaks in part to the impatient urgency this person feels to have his or her desires satisfied as quickly as possible. My toddler illustrates this form of the aesthetic when, for example, he hears the word *chocolate* and expects to receive it at once or else throws a fit. Kierkegaard illustrates this stage through the character of Don Juan, who has an insatiable appetite for women and gives little thought to the moment after his conquest concludes. The very thought of a women leads him to act on his desires almost immediately. Two problems complicate this individual's life. First is what Freud called the reality principle, the consequences of life lived according to the criteria of immediate pleasure seeking. If I gave my child chocolate or ice cream or cake whenever he asked for it, there would be dire consequences for his health, not to mention his character. Obviously Don Juan's lifestyle exemplifies how out of control such a position can be, as one clearly can discern major risks to one's physical and emotional health, not to mention the vulnerability of such a lifestyle simply to bad luck or competition from other equally skilled bachelors. This form of existence is not risk free, even if it is commitment free. Second, after a period of time living according to one's immediate desires the aesthete faces the prospect of boredom. Conquests of the newest or the greatest begin to resemble one another, and one recognizes that the realization of these desires is no longer satisfying.

The reflective aesthete seems to recognize the limits of this sort of life and with great cleverness and a bit of patience decides to vary the kinds of desires he or she has, rather than aim for more of the same. In the pseudonymous essay "Rotation of Crops," a reflective aesthete decides that the best way to avoid the problem of boredom is to do what farmers do to keep their soil rich—vary what one plants. Instead of moving around corn, soybeans and wheat, the reflective aesthete tries different people, different careers, different hobbies to see what they will yield. As soon as the fear of boredom looms on the horizon, one moves on to the next thing, harvests the next field over. This aesthete is reflective in that he or she is more creative, more industrious in keeping boredom, which he humorously calls "the root of all evil," at bay. Similar to the immediate aesthete, however, reflective aesthetes have no real, enduring commitments—whether to people or to ideals. The objects of their interest, whether a person or a project, are of instrumental value only, sought for the good feeling they produce and little else. The reflective aesthete's tools to stave off boredom are clearly more sophisticated than the immediate aesthete's, but ultimately they face a similar consequence of failing to provide sustained satisfaction or meaning to a human life. Viewing both aesthetes through the lens of the categories of despair, it is possible to say both could suffer from the despair of finitude in that both lack any sense of the infinite qualities of human existence.[13] The reason for this owes to

---

[13]There is no direct correspondence between life spheres and forms of despair, and so one could also imagine an aesthete who suffers from despair of infinitude.

the inability to appreciate that what often brings the most fulfillment to human lives are the commitments to others or to God that lead us beyond ourselves, our finite concerns and our personal preferences.

"You can't reason with a fool," and the same goes with aesthetic existence. There is no knock-down, drag-out argument that when properly constructed and eloquently communicated works to prove to the aesthete that there is more to life than what this sphere affords.[14] Part of the reason for this can be found in the proverb quoted above; appealing to someone through reason when his or her reason is subservient to feeling or to desire is a strategy doomed to failure. But even if there were strong arguments available, the problems with aesthetic existence do not lie solely in one's reasoning or intellect, but with the heart, desires and character. The aesthete's passions just as much as the aesthete's reasoning powers are in need of a moral and spiritual transformation. If the aesthete takes a step forward it will be through a personal recognition of the futility of basing life on the not-so-solid foundation of momentary enjoyment and satisfaction, and this recognition will reflect not simply a maturation of thought but of the emotions and the will.

Two paths are possible at this point. First, one may take up a position Kierkegaard interestingly calls "irony," a kind of middle zone between the aesthetic and ethical stages. This somewhat melancholic position notices the shortcomings of hedonistic, superficial lifestyles so typical of the aesthetic. Such a move signifies an advance past the aesthetic, though it is only a midpoint to the next stage. The reason is that the ironist may also loathe the idea of making the sorts of commitments that the subsequent spheres, the ethical and religious lives, demand. The other possibility is that an aesthete who comes to the end of his or her rope may transition directly to what Kierkegaard calls ethical existence, and this occurs through a passionate choice—something that should not surprise us given the strong emphasis on freedom discussed thus far. In describing the choice as one of passion, Kierkegaard conveys that the will really is the problem with the aesthetic, not false beliefs. When

---

[14]The notion that there is no rock-solid argument available to prove that ethical or religious existence is higher than aesthetic existence explains one reason Kierkegaard has been labeled an irrationalist and a subjectivist.

the will is transformed and desires what is good or at least what is better, this is indicative of the transformation of one's deep cares and motivation—one's passions.

Although the ethical and religious stages are distinguished in Kierkegaard's developmental scheme, it is important to note that they are not mutually exclusive categories. By calling one sphere ethical and the other religious Kierkegaard is not suggesting the religious sphere lacks ethics or is unethical, nor does he mean that those in the ethical stage are by definition irreligious. Ethical existence simply connotes a way of life dominated by the recognition and fulfillment of one's commitment and duties to others, and while clearly many who live this way are religious, certainly many who do are *not* religious. In contrast to the aesthete, the ethical individual has a longer-term view of time. In terms of the varieties of despair, the ethical person is less likely than the aesthete to have finitude's despair because the ethical person recognizes the infinite (or quasi-infinite) aspects of human existence, such as one's lifelong commitment to a spouse. Whereas Don Juan has no concern about the morning after his present affair, the ethical person acts with consideration of how present decisions will inform and affect one's future. Commitment to projects and people beyond oneself and a sense of time beyond the present moment contribute to the formation of a coherent, unified self. From the perspective of the ethical, the aesthetic self is fragmented, lacking unity as a whole life. Kierkegaard voices ethical existence through the pseudonym Judge William, who speaks passionately of the importance of commitment in marriage and carrying out one's duties in society. Though it is true that one can remain in the sphere of the aesthetic just like a Don Juan, and even though there are no proofs that guarantee the conversion of the aesthete's thought and will, Kierkegaard clearly illustrates the shortcomings of the aesthetic in part through placing Judge William in conversation with an aesthete. The judge attempts to convince the aesthete not only that the ethical life is superior and more fulfilling, but that it is better even when judged by the aesthete's own criteria. If pleasure, love and satisfaction are what the aesthete wants, he can find it all in marriage, the judge argues. Though at times it appears the judge overstates the bliss and benefits of marriage and of ethical existence, he properly diagnoses the aesthetic as a way of existing that leads finally to despair.

As good as it sounds, the ethical life faces its own problems and is not itself exempt from despair. Ethical existence is characterized by adhering to one's moral commitments and obligations, living the life of the dutiful citizen. However, no amount of commitment entails perfect obedience to the moral law; the ethical person will at some point or another fail to live up to the high standard of ethical existence. A dilemma confronts the ethical individual at this point. On the one hand, the individual self is the cause of the problem—it is no one else's fault that one has failed to observe one's duty. And yet ethical existence offers no solution to such failure outside the self and its own effort-filled striving. Kierkegaard calls this "the deepest ethical self-contradiction." The appropriate response to moral failure is to repent, and yet repentance assumes unethical behavior. It appears the ethical stage will soon be an empty set—a group with no members able to live up to the ethical ideal or standard they affirm. Kierkegaard summarizes the problem: "As soon as sin is introduced, ethics runs aground precisely on repentance, for repentance is the highest ethical expression but precisely as such the deepest ethical self-contradiction" (FT 86).

On her own the ethical person lacks the resources to close what John Hare calls the moral gap, the space between one's ethical ideal and one's actual living according to that ideal.[15] What is necessary is divine assistance, intervention from the outside. Yet those in this sphere, even if they believe in God, tend to see God as little more than a being whose expectations for their lives are coterminous with the expectations of society. To say it differently, those in the ethical sphere tend to relate to God on their (or their culture's) own terms and thereby unconsciously assume their own efforts (or their culture's conception of duty) can bring about a solution to their sin. Additional moral striving, doing a better job of pulling up one's ethical bootstraps, promises of future perfection, will compensate for errors I have made. On this view, Kierkegaard says, God becomes "an invisible vanishing point, an impotent thought" (FT 59).

---

[15]See John Hare, *The Moral Gap: Kantian Ethics, Human Limits, and God's Assistance* (New York: Oxford University Press, 1996).

One might begin to notice a resemblance between this ethical individual and the Pelagian perspective described in chapter two—willpower, effort and committedness ultimately lead to my flourishing. On the ethical view God is not so much a distinct divine being capable of judgment and forgiveness, justice and restoration, but a therapeutic tool that serves the needs of those who feel bad about their behavior.

In moving to the third sphere, the religious, Kierkegaard does not mean to suggest that ethics is left behind. Sometimes he speaks of the "ethico-religious," implying that any religious conception of life necessarily includes ethical living. Still, he is clear that contra the liberal theological view, religion and religious existence cannot be *reduced* to ethics. As we saw in chapter two, in Christianity the truth is not Christ's teaching but rather Christ himself. Religious existence for Kierkegaard is fundamentally about turning to the incarnate God for assistance. He divides this sphere into two forms, a general sort of Religiousness (A) and Christianity (B). Religiousness A is a mode of existence compatible with different religious viewpoints and is the mark of a religiously humbled and mature person, of someone who recognizes the need for God's help.[16] As such, this sphere is characterized by three passion-filled expressions—resignation, suffering and guilt. The person in this stage recognizes the need to properly order all finite creations as they relate to the infinite Creator, to recognize their relative value compared to God. Since humans tend to make idols out of almost anything, resignation is a painful process characterized further by suffering. As finite creatures we are deeply invested in finite goods, be they people or careers or possessions. And although God calls us to resign all things before him, we will likely fail in this task and thus experience a particularly religious form of guilt. Resignation, suffering and guilt do not exhaust Christian existence but are certainly part of it, and thus those of other religious traditions can and do experience these features of religious life.

---

[16]Just as irony marks the boundary between aesthetic and ethical existence, humor marks the boundary between ethical and religious existence. The person who takes up this stance recognizes the shortcomings of ethical life, how one cannot overcome one's moral failings by oneself. In a sense, this person "laughs" at others' attempts at moral perfection and recognizes universal human failure at this endeavor. Yet, this person—suffering perhaps from despair of necessity— lacks the hope that in one's own life it is possible for God to rectify the moral gap.

Kierkegaard understands Christianity's distinctiveness from other religions (i.e., Religiousness A) primarily in terms of sin (described above) and faith in Jesus Christ (described in chapter two). Thus he calls the A form of religiousness *immanent*, that which lies within the grasp of human reason to understand, and Christianity he calls *transcendent* in that it is revealed religion. Faith in Jesus Christ as the God-human is more often than not offensive to human reason *and also* to the human desire for autonomy or self-rule, and for this reason, it is a doubly challenging, though in Kierkegaard's mind true, solution to the difficulties of human existence.

IMPLICATIONS FOR CHRISTIAN SELFHOOD

Before proceeding to a fuller discussion of Christian existence in the final two chapters, let us briefly apply Kierkegaard's developmental psychology to our attempts to live out that existence. We might begin by asking whether the following words about his Christian contemporaries seem to apply in our own day: "Basically they have their lives in other categories, which gives them a deceptive security while they busy themselves with and concern themselves about the religious" (BA 105). To what extent do those of us who claim Christian faith live in the categories of the aesthetic or the ethical?

Let us begin with the *Christian aesthete*. With the aesthetic comes the reminder that where our treasure is, there our heart is as well (Mt 6:21; Lk 12:34). Even if one is not a womanizer like Don Juan or Johannes the seducer, one's treasure could be in shallow relationships or the opinions others hold about one's social network status. It could easily lie in one's career and the achievement of accolades or benefits associated with work. One's treasure might be less pronounced than a job and might lie more subtly in habits of self-medication so prevalent in contemporary culture. Driven by what feels good or helps us cope with stress, the *aesthetic Christian* might be inordinately drawn toward the need to be entertained. Perhaps one hops from church to church or small group to small group as the wind blows, seeking a momentary spiritual high without planting deeper roots in a spiritual community. Importantly, wanting to feel good and to experience pleasure do not nor should not dissipate with genuine Christian faith, but they are basic dimensions of human life that are radically transformed as they are oriented toward higher goods such as a relation to God and genuine, committed care for one's neighbor.

Marked by fragmentation, aesthetic existence lacks the integration of one's beliefs and passions with one's past, present and future. For example, if the aesthete fails to learn from past mistakes and subsequently has no sense of how to improve his or her own future, then the *Christian aesthete* might be identified as one who gets in spiritual ruts—cycles of sin or disobedience—endlessly failing to move forward. In the repulsive words of King Solomon, such a "Christian" returns like the dog to its vomit as he does to his foolish ways (Prov 26:11). And in a sense such Christian folly is more pernicious because it is loosely costumed by the appearance of faith: Christian-speak and church attendance. At the root of phony religiosity is selfishness and solipsism, as the Christian aesthete refuses not only the call of God to put away sin but the convicting power of God's people, who might speak words of truth and encouragement and support the wavering soul. If in our most honest moments we discover we are little more than pleasure seekers who live for the moment and refuse the intrusion of those who would call us to account for our out-of-sync lives, then our self-identification as Christian may be little more than a self-deceiving label to comfort our souls and justify our superficial existence.

What about the Christian stuck in the ethical sphere? While being dutiful citizens who recognize and seek to fulfill commitments to others is commendable and certainly consistent with Christian ethical behavior, the strong sense of pride that often accompanies sparkling citizenship can easily result in spiritual smugness, like the Pharisee with his holier-than-thou prayer (Lk 18:11). The Christian who inhabits this sphere thinks that the ultimate difference between Christians and everyone else is how well Christians behave, how good they are and thus how different they are from others. In one sense this conviction is not altogether unbiblical, as Jesus indeed says that trees are known by the fruit they produce (Lk 6:44). It is reasonable and important to expect that Christians will behave ethically and that their good behavior will serve as a distinguishing witness to others. But at this point the *ethical Christian's* views really are no different from the ethical views of most world religions. Every major world religion affirms a code of conduct and the importance of doing one's duty, and as many scholars have pointed out, to a large degree these codes of conduct resemble one another. As we saw above, however, Kierkegaard believes that Christian existence is decisively marked by nearly the opposite of what the ethical Christian supposes. Christian existence is distinguished by an explicit confession that at the end of the day one *fails* to fulfill the ethical demands on one's life. Moreover, Christian existence confesses that the solution to one's failure has to come from God. Thus the fruits one should expect of Christians are repentance, humility and trust rather than pride and self-confidence.

The *ethical Christian* position can also be seen in the very prevalent civic Christianity of American culture that tends to understand Christian faith in a superficial way as more or less complying with rules like the Ten Commandments or voting for one or another social or moral program identified as Christian.[17] Such civic Christianity demotes the two absolutely unique features of Christianity, according to Kierkegaard: deep and personal familiarity with one's own sin, and trust and rest in Jesus Christ for forgiveness of that sin. It subsequently exchanges these distinctives for a distilled version of Christianity reduced to externals. When behavior, outward appearance and societally approved Christian practice are central, one might ponder the degree to which one's Christianity is stuck in the ethical sphere.

If as Christians we struggle living in these other categories, then any attempt to follow the biblical command to share the Christian message with others will be misguided and misleading. Let us turn, then, to the topic of the Christian's witness to the world, a witness marked by uniquely Christian categories of existence.

QUESTIONS FOR REFLECTION

1. What does it mean for my daily life that God has *lovingly* created me?

2. With which form(s) of despair do I most identify, and why?

3. Kierkegaard writes: "Basically they have their lives in other categories, which gives them a deceptive security while they busy themselves with and concern themselves about the religious" (BA 105). Is this an accurate description of me? My family? My church?

4. To what extent am I an aesthetic Christian?

---

[17]These programs occur on both sides of the political aisle.

CHRISTIAN WITNESS

What one's life proclaims is a hundred thousand times more powerfully effective than what one's mouth proclaims.

JUDGE FOR YOURSELF!, 131-32

THE CHURCH HAS ALWAYS BEEN an outward-facing body, imitating its outward-facing Savior, whose arms symbolically extend on the cross in embrace of a world in need of saving. Christians are *on mission*, therefore, and must thoughtfully explore how best to convey what they consider *good* news for the world. Though sharing the gospel involves proclaiming some facts about God and God's relation to the world, it also includes demonstrating how those facts have impacted one's own life. The Christian gospel is good news *for you* and *for me, for this person* and *for that one*. In the previous chapters we addressed two sets of those transformative facts— in chapter two those concerning God in Christ and his saving grace, and in chapter three those concerning humans and their sin. The final two chapters flesh out how these facts take shape in human lives. While chapter five explores the Christian ethic of love that follows from the gospel making its way into a human life, here we address fundamental issues related to the communication of these facts to the world.

DIRECT-INDIRECT COMMUNICATION

Kierkegaard is widely recognized as a master of indirect communication, and he has earned this reputation largely because of his employment of pseudonyms, his taking up of multiple perspectives that reflect radically different worldviews and his use of indirect literary devices such as irony, humor and satire. All of these things have endeared him especially to those who study literature and deconstruction in particular. Interestingly, however, within Kierkegaard scholarship attention to these features as the primary markers of Kierkegaard's indirect methods has almost entirely obscured what he himself claimed was the primary feature of an indirect communication. As we will see, this feature has enormous implications for Christian communication.

In a series of unpublished lectures on communication Kierkegaard repeatedly refers to indirect communication as a *communication of capability* (JP 1:651). Indirect communication is therefore evocative communication— communication that aims to draw out of its recipient some response or another. Kierkegaard distinguishes indirect communication with direct communication, which he calls a *communication of knowledge*. The difference between the two can be seen through a humorous illustration:

> A sergeant in the National Guard says to a recruit, "You, there, stand up straight."
>
> Recruit: "Sure enough."
>
> Sergeant: "Yes, and don't talk during the drill."
>
> Recruit: "All right, I won't if you'll just tell me."
>
> Sergeant: "What the devil! You are not supposed to talk during drill!"
>
> Recruit: "Well, don't get so mad. If I know I'm not supposed to, I'll quit talking during your drill" (JP 1:649 [#272])

The recruit, who seems to be hearing but not listening, mistakes a communication of capability for a communication of knowledge. He hears the sergeant's words and is able to recite them back; he fails, however, to recognize that they are not simply for him to hear or to memorize but for him to *enact*. The sergeant's command requires action, performance, an existential, not merely cognitive response. As an indirect communication, the command insists that he *do* something.

As a Christian missionary to Christians, Kierkegaard believes that the problem in Christendom is not knowledge of the Christian faith but acting according to that knowledge. Like the dense recruit, Christians claim to understand Christianity without recognizing its effect on their lives. This, then, explains what Kierkegaard is doing both in the pseudonymous writings but also the signed, religious writings. In the former he aims to awaken a decision and response in the lives of nominal Christians who find themselves attracted to lifestyles and worldviews like the aesthetic or the ethical that are not actually Christian. And in the latter writings he aims to evoke from his reader specifically Christian virtues or actions, such as hopefulness or courage or trust in God. Although indirect methods can serve different sorts of missional purposes, in all cases they aim at drawing out of the other some actual response. Contrasted with direct communication, the goal goes far beyond the communication of some piece of knowledge.

A second distinction follows the first: whereas direct communication is conveyed through the *medium of imagination*, indirect communication is conveyed through the *medium of actuality* (JP 1:651). In other words, direct communications occur through the transmission of ideas. Indirect communications, on the other hand, take place in actuality—in lives. For this reason, oftentimes the best forms of indirect communication are nonverbal. We might imagine, for example, that had the sergeant not spoken to the recruit but angrily and silently gotten up in his face, he might have had success evoking the actual response of silence in the recruit. To use a similar example, sometimes a stern look at one's child evokes a desired response more effectively than uttering the same command for the umpteenth time. Importantly, Kierkegaard recognizes the irony of discussing these matters through words (rather than through actions), and he also recognizes that as brilliant as his books are, they are not necessarily the most effective tool of indirect communication. Indirect communication through lives rather than words is far more gripping and possibly more effective, and in the case of Christianity, appropriate:

> To teach in actuality that the truth is ridiculed, etc., means to teach it as one ridiculed and scoffed at himself. To teach poverty in actuality means to teach it as one who is himself poor. . . . To that extent all instruction ends in a kind of silence; for when I existentially express it, it is not necessary for my speaking to be audible (JP 1:286 [#653]).

Actions speak louder than words. Kierkegaard would simply add the following: (1) this is all the more true when the words have become so familiar that they've lost their meaning and (2) indirect communication through actions can more successfully draw actions out of the one who receives the communication.

From what we have said to this point it might appear that Kierkegaard advocates indirect communication over direct communication. In one sense this is true. As I have suggested above, almost all of his writings are committed not to trying to convince readers of true propositions but to drawing out of them some sort of existential response, whether it be a decision of faith or specifically ethical or religious actions. Despite this strong emphasis, however, and despite the fact that Kierkegaard maintains that communicating "Blessed are those who are persecuted" through actuality is more compelling than merely preaching the relevant Bible passage, specifically Christian communication is different. Kierkegaard labels Christian communication *direct-indirect*. It is direct insofar as it communicates truth claims—doctrines like the incarnation, for example. Christian witness necessarily includes the communication of these doctrines as knowledge claims the recipient must wrestle with and ultimately accept should he or she come to faith. But that is not all—the Christian witness is indirect as well, since it does not stop with assent to those beliefs but looks to the implications of those beliefs on one's life. There is a second reason why the Christian witness will make use of indirect methods. If one's audience is overly familiar with Christianity, as was Kierkegaard's, then clearly what is missing is not theological knowledge. In that case what is needed is communication that seeks to evoke from cultural Christians actions that are actually Christian. *This* is what Kierkegaard believes to be precisely lacking not just in the Christians of his day but in pastors specifically.

PROBLEMS WITH PASTORS

When Kierkegaard was a boy he was asked what he would most like to be, and his response was *en gaffel*, a fork: "Then I could 'spear' anything I wanted on the dinner table."[1] It is no surprise that the nickname stuck

---

[1]The story is recounted by Troels Frederick Troels-Lund, quoted in Bruce Kirmmse's *Encounters with Kierkegaard: A Life as Seen by His Contemporaries* (Princeton, NJ: Princeton University Press, 1996), 3.

given the reputation he would earn as a sharp and quick-witted critic and interlocutor. He had his favorite targets; among them were *Privatdocents*, something akin to graduate assistants or university lecturers, and pastors. While he jabbed at the former mostly over their presumptuousness as it related to philosophical speculation, his attack on the pastorate was far more thorough and devastating. Undoubtedly this was due to what was at stake, in his mind. Pastors, Kierkegaard believed, were supposed to be witnesses to the truth of the gospel above all else.

A pair of anecdotes illustrate Kierkegaard's concerns about the clergy. In *Fear and Trembling* he describes a parson who "in quite ordinary terms" tells his congregation the story of Abraham's near-sacrifice of Isaac (FT 22). Most of us—Christians or not—are familiar with the story: God calls Abraham to sacrifice his son. Abraham demonstrates obedience to God and just before the deed is done an angel stays his hand and provides a ram for the sacrifice instead. It is a familiar story the parson has retold many times, and perhaps for that reason he is entirely unmoved by its weighty claims: that God would command a man to kill his teenage son for no apparent reason and—what's more startling—the man would be willing to obey. Not until one of the parson's parishioners decides he too should follow the example of Abraham and sacrifice *his* son does the parson's pulse elevate beyond a dead man's, and he subsequently excoriates the parishioner for even considering such an action. Kierkegaard writes of the parson, "The mistake was simply that he had not known what he was saying" (FT 23). Familiarity with the story bred apathy to its meaning and implications; the preacher became detached from his proclamation, unmoved by the witness of his own faith.

Kierkegaard spins another tale of a recent seminary graduate, a soon-to-be pastor who seeks a prestigious church appointment with the utmost effort and determination, as though his whole life hinged on the outcome. After devoting what appears to be inordinate energy to this pursuit he finally gets his wish. The young seminary graduate is installed as pastor and for his first sermon he preaches from Matthew 6: "Seek first the kingdom of God." The sermon is enthralling, and the parishioners are happy to have gotten their man. Amid the bliss of the moment, however, no one seems to notice that in his pursuit of a job the graduate ironically and tragically fails to seek first God's kingdom himself. The parson and the young seminary graduate lack integrity; Kierkegaard concludes there is no "agreement . . . between the preacher's life and his sermon" (JFY 112).

Kierkegaard writes scores of paragraphs critical of pastors under whose watch the church itself is disintegrating. He points out the following problems:

- Pastors' lives do not reflect their sermons.
- Pastors do not really mean what they preach, so that preaching "jams the lock on imitation" (FSE 261).
- Pastors preach watered-down drivel, and thus they are dishonest about the gospel—its claims and its demands on human life.
- The pastorate is a professional job no different from any other in law, business, medicine and so on. The implications are that some are drawn to the "trade" for secular reasons and thus some pastors have gotten themselves in the wrong business.
- In their sermons pastors promote the view that doctrine matters more than the imitation of Christ; faith is intellectualized.
- Pastors do not understand the world in which they live (i.e., non-Christian forms of existence), nor do they care to, and thus their message is largely irrelevant.
- Pastors offend, but for the wrong sorts of reasons.

Given all this, Kierkegaard writes, "we should not hesitate to preach against Christianity in Christian sermons" (WL 198). This sounds funny, but Kierkegaard is not contradicting himself here. What goes by the name of Christianity so often is something else, and thus true Christian preaching must be self-critical as much as it is critical of easy and obvious targets like "the world" or "the flesh" or "pagans."

Though one could write a dissertation on Kierkegaard's digressions about pastors, we will draw our focus instead on a broader conception of the church's witness as understood in the calling on *all* Christians to follow and proclaim Christ and his kingdom. As a Reformed thinker, Kierkegaard does not shy away from the duty on all followers of Christ to be priests and also to be witnesses to the gospel.

WITNESSING TO THE WAY, TRUTH AND LIFE

Contrary to the self-understanding of many Christians, all who follow Jesus are called to be witnesses. Of course the idea of communicating Christian truth to others frightens many of us, but if Christian communication is partly indirect—perhaps nonverbal, definitely existential—then we might wonder whether the church has failed to think as broadly as it should about witness as something *lived*. In a sense, far more frightening than reciting the Roman road or Four Spiritual Laws is living the truths proclaimed therein. And yet, Kierkegaard argues, "the essential sermon is one's own existence" (JP 1:460 [#1056]).

The truth is a life. In *Concluding Unscientific Postscript* and in his journals Kierkegaard augments our understanding of Christian communication by describing Christianity itself as an "existence-communication." This odd designation means (1) Christianity is something lived and (2) Christianity is something communicated (or witnessed to) through life, or existence. This implies: (1) Christianity is *not* something primarily to think about or to ponder, nor (2) is it something primarily communicated (or witnessed to) through words. We have noted how Christianity must also be communicated through the verbal proclamation of the gospel—directly—as Paul emphatically claims in Romans 10. The main idea for the moment, however, is that whatever Christianity is, it is a *lived* thing and not primarily a *known* thing.[2] Kierkegaard claims this is the case for Jesus: "Truth in the sense in which Christ is the truth is not a sum of statements, not a definition etc., but a life" (PC 205). Likewise, this is the case for Jesus' followers: "The being of truth is the redoubling of truth within yourself, within me, within him, that your life, my life, his life expresses the truth" (PC 205). To redouble truth is to take what you hear, to take what you have been taught, and put it into practice, appropriate it in life. To re*double* truth is to *duplicate* beliefs into godly actions and spiritual emotions. For the Christian, it is to imitate Christ.

To redouble the truth that we are to forgive as we have been forgiven (Col 3:13) means that the belief one has about forgiveness, the knowledge

---

[2]"Primarily" is an important qualifier here. Christianity is indeed something known (see the discussion in the subsequent paragraph). Importantly, however, *knowing* Christian truths does not exhaust the meaning of Christianity or Christian belief or Christian life or Christian witness.

one possesses from reading Scripture, makes its way from the mind into the heart (emotions) and life (actions) when one has been offended. For Kierkegaard, what follows from understanding Christian truth as *a life* is that if one does not *live* according to the beliefs one holds about forgiveness, one more or less demonstrates one really does not *know* the truth one claims to believe. "Being the truth is identical with knowing the truth" (PC 205). When one forgives the offender, when one *embodies* or *incarnates* or *lives* forgiveness, one demonstrates true understanding or true knowledge of Colossians 3:13. But the opposite does not follow, at least in the thinnest sense of knowledge. Memorizing the verse, preaching on it or telling others of its truth does not imply one lives or embodies forgiveness. In such a position, "I am untruthfully outside of myself" (PC 206). In other words, when Christian truth is merely held true as a bit of knowledge one would give assent to, but does not find its way into one's life, one is spiritually ignorant. Such a disconnect between knowledge and action demonstrates a deeper fracture in the self, a dis-integration that the New Testament calls hypocrisy. Jesus himself directly addresses such existential incongruity: "Not everyone who says to me, 'Lord, Lord,' will enter the kingdom of heaven, but only the one who does the will of my Father in heaven" (Mt 7:21). The commonly held grudge against religious hypocrites is no less than Kierkegaard's point here—that failure to appropriate one's beliefs gives the skeptic strong reason to doubt those beliefs are meaningful in a person's life (true in Kierkegaard's stipulated sense), which subsequently gives the critic strong reason to doubt those beliefs are true (in an everyday sense).

The truth is the way. Economists, people considering moving to take a new job and Americans in general concern themselves with quality of life, which they often understand in terms of some financial measure. If Christianity involves living in accordance with the truth of Jesus Christ, then quality of life for Christians means something entirely different. Quality Christian existence takes as its starting point the requirement on each Christian to follow Christ himself or herself. Accordingly, while I can inherit a decent financial quality of life from my parents, the same is not true when it comes to faith, which cannot be passed down to one's children like church pews, the lake house or detached earlobes.

"In relation to truth there is no abridgement that leaves out the acquiring of it. . . . Every generation and everyone in the generation must essentially begin from the beginning" (PC 203). Neither mom nor dad can follow Christ for me, nor can one's piety go into the bank for the kids.[3]

Kierkegaard speculates that one reason why Christians of his day fail to view their faith as a path for them to walk themselves is rooted in what we referred to in chapter two as the argument from Christendom. The thinking goes as follows: given the enormously successful results of the Christian religion over nearly two millennia, we can assume the truth of the religion and gladly accept the beliefs that come with it.[4] We can stand on the shoulders of giants—church fathers, saints, theologians, pastors and spiritual mentors—and leave the spiritual heavy lifting to them. However, if the truth is the way, if being a person of Christian faith includes walking a certain path, then such an argument does not work.

To speak of Christian truth as a life and as a way means that the appropriate self-concept for a Christian seeking to follow Christ is, as noted above, *becoming*, not *arrived*. Kierkegaard helpfully illustrates the point by contrasting Christian faith with the invention of gunpowder. Let us suppose it took someone twenty years to invent gunpowder. Whether it took twenty years, twenty minutes or twenty millennia, once the knowledge is attained—once it has *arrived*—it can be passed on rather quickly to someone else. This means that *how* one ended up with the knowledge to make gunpowder—the process, the hard work, the energy and labor, the time—is inconsequential to the fact *that* one ended up with knowledge to make gunpowder. The fact that the person who expended the time, energy and money to discover gunpowder might feel the process was essential makes little difference. The *how* of technological discoveries is in many cases remarkably inconsequential, so much so that

---

[3]N. T. Wright makes a parallel point about the reading of Scripture: "Each generation must do its own fresh historically grounded reading, because each generation needs to *grow* up, not simply to *look* up the right answers and remain in an infantile condition." "Do We Need a Historical Adam?" in *Surprised by Scripture* (New York: Harper One, 2015), 30.

[4]All Kierkegaard means here is its wild popularity. Christianity is the largest religion in the world—nearly one-third of all people identify as Christian. Certainly there are other results of which the church would be less proud.

even if discoveries are made accidentally they are nevertheless welcomed and exploited. Thus, "If he who invented [gunpowder] invented it one evening when he was going home drunk from a party by stumbling over a gutter plank, the way is entirely a matter of indifference" (PC 208). Human civilization has made a number of accelerated strides forward by one person ripping off the sweat-filled labors of others who came before.

By contrast, if the truth is the way as in Christianity, the way "cannot be shortened or drop out"—it is *essential* to the truth (PC 207). One cannot substitute anything for following Jesus, with all the energy, hard work and time it requires. Following Jesus cannot be shortened to a ten-step procedure abridged by a guru; no computer app can make it less rigorous or painful. One can thus see how interdependent the *truth as life* and the *truth as way* are. If we think of Christianity merely as a set of true statements or facts about God that, once accepted, make us Christian, then the process of following Jesus that follows the belief is omitted. However, if we construe those truth claims as claims about and on our lives, then we must acknowledge that following Christ is an ongoing task undertaken throughout one's entire life.

Kierkegaard's thoughts here are undoubtedly tied to his cultural context, in which Christian faith was the default cultural and religious position, and one's birth and baptismal certificates were more or less the same thing. Thus its relevance for American Christians may vary based on how culturally rooted Christian faith is in a given place. It is far more likely, for example, that one can be a default Christian, so to speak, in the Bible-belt South than in the Northeast, in certain pockets of the Midwest than certain pockets of the Northwest. Thus the advantages of living in a place that seems more friendly to Christianity might have the reverse effect of making the *way* of Christ-following all the more difficult to discern and carry out. Such are the ills of what Kierkegaard refers to as established Christendom.

The way is self-denial. In Matthew 4, when Jesus first calls Simon Peter and Andrew to come follow him, the *way* commences when they leave their jobs; they drop their fishing nets and choose instead to fish for people. This opening act of following Jesus earns them the name *disciples* or *followers*. In the ensuing narrative up to Matthew 16 the *way* grows more difficult, and in Matthew 16:24 Jesus reaffirms his initial call—"deny yourself"—but then makes explicit the logical end of self-denial for his sake: taking up one's cross. The kind of self-denial that leads one to quit one's job for Christ has as its natural end quitting one's life for Christ. In settings where Christianity is strongly established culturally and/or politically, where it is viewed as a "triumphant" institution, such self-denial, he argues, is unlikely if not impossible. For although the masses may together profess their faith, this does not entail the masses deny themselves for the sake of Christ.

Because Jesus tells his followers to take up their cross and follow him, Kierkegaard contends that the church will not be triumphant until it abides together with Christ in eternity. On this side of things, conversely, Christians must be drawn to Jesus *in his lowliness*, and lowliness is the last thing that comes to mind when the average person considers ideas like triumph and victory. Jesus' invitation to would-be followers prioritizes his agenda of loving God and God's world more than one loves oneself and one's own agendas. To say yes to the invitation, to submit in obedience to Christ, includes following his example. What sort of example did Christ leave for us, what sort of way did he traverse? Rather than ascend to positions of religious or political power he "emptied himself, taking the form of a slave" (Phil 2:7). Though Jesus could have called legions of angels to his side when Satan tempted him and when he hung on the cross, "he humbled himself and became obedient to the point of death" (Phil 2:8). Thus, Kierkegaard concludes, those who follow his voice are called to nothing less.

The way of the Christian life is therefore a way of self-denial or death to self, as Paul describes it in Romans 6. On any account such a path is one most of us in our honest moments would rather avoid for any number of reasons. For one, the way of self-denial calls for deep, inward struggle with the parts of our selves that would rather be left alone to their own way. If one knows one must forgive an offender, but it feels better to hold a grudge or it is simply difficult to forgive, then the process by which one follows Jesus through forgiveness involves deep personal struggle, an inward battle in which one submits to the pattern and command of Christ.

A second reason we find the life of self-denial challenging pertains to how such a life is received by those who do not share Christian faith. Consider forgiveness once again. Ours is a media-consuming society that perversely exposes sin and rarely forgets it. In such a context, when one lover is betrayed by another but then Christianly extends forgiveness, it is not uncommon for such behavior to be met by others not only with surprise but with censure. Or take any number of publicized criminal acts that all but demand our unforgiving outcry. The way of self-denial, the way of Christ, which operates not by the world's conception of judgment, grudge holding and vengeance but by the gospel's claims "he who is without sin cast the first stone" and "forgive as you've been forgiven," leaves the Christian who appropriates that truth vulnerable to scoffing, insults and disrespect. Kierkegaard calls the suffering of the one whose personal self-denial becomes public in such a way Christianity's "decisive qualification" (PC 222). In *Works of Love* Kierkegaard speaks of the "double danger" of Christian love, which mirrors the dual challenge of inward and outward struggle. As we will note in chapter five, Christ's command to love our neighbor disrupts our self-loving existence, but then when we are finally obedient it has the potential to disrupt our existence in the world. For self-denial nearly always makes the non-Christian feel badly about his or her own self-absorbed existence, which is subsequently processed through anger, judgment and ridicule.

Given this understanding of the Christian's witness as a life and a way of self-denial, it may be apparent why Kierkegaard conceives of the true church not as triumphant but as "militant." A militant church is a church of warriors and fighters whose lives are characterized by struggle against the sinful nature, who long to follow Christ and know that to do so is to share in the "fellowship of his sufferings" (Phil 3:10 KJV). Importantly, to speak of the church as militant does not entail a wholesale antagonism toward secular culture, as some Christians suppose. Rather, it is to recognize the never-ceasing fight against placing ourselves above Christ and his reign in our lives and on earth. Only in eternity will the struggle end, and thus Kierkegaard stipulates that the church triumphant is not the church established culturally or politically in a society, but rather a church whose Christians no longer struggle with sin but freely and wholly follow Christ. Although in one sense—salvation—victory was won on the cross, in the sense described here—sanctification—victory lies ahead. As Paul writes, "Not that I have already obtained this or have already reached the goal; but I press on to make it my own, because Christ Jesus has made me his own" (Phil 3:12). In the meantime, the Christian life of self-denial powerfully expresses the gospel in action, and to this witness of faith some will likewise respond in faith, and others will not.

VARIETIES OF RELIGIOUS OFFENSE

It is hard to dispute the claim that almost nothing offends like religion offends. Most Christians can attest to at least a few of the following experiences: unknowingly offending someone else because of one's Christian faith; knowingly doing so; being offended by those hostile to one's faith; being offended by fellow Christians. Some fundamentalists are known for going out of their way to be offensive, and often their offensiveness is utterly indiscriminate. The thinking is, if I'm not being offensive I'm not preaching the gospel. After all, to "those who are perishing" knowledge of God is "an aroma that brings death" (2 Cor 2:15-16 NIV). Conversely, others go out of their way to avoid being offensive. We find this in both conservative evangelical circles in the form of seeker-sensitive ecclesiologies, for example, and in the mainline liberal church, which can come across as trying to play down features of Christianity that distinguish it from other faiths. Kierkegaard puts the opposing approaches this way:

> Christianity can falsely be made so severe that human nature must revolt against it in order to cast it or thrust it away. But Christianity can also be made so lenient or flavored with sweetness that all attempts to perk up the appetite and give people a taste for it with demonstrations and reasons are futile and end up making people disgusted with it. (JFY 203)

The question before us is how to be faithful to Scripture in offending no more but also no less than we must. How, precisely, does the gospel offend, and from that, how does our witness to the gospel offend? Anything more than that may not be useful or loving, and anything less than that may not be faithful or obedient.

Nonessential (moral) offense. In *Practice in Christianity* Kierkegaard distinguishes between offense that is essentially Christian and that which is not. Essentially Christian offense occurs when one is offended quite simply by one particular feature of Christian faith that is exclusive, hence essential, to Christian faith—specifically, the idea that God became a human being in Jesus Christ. While one might be offended by Judaism or by Islam, however that might go, one could not possibly be offended in *this* manner since neither Judaism nor Islam shares the belief that God became a human being in Jesus Christ. Of course the Old and New Testaments (and every major world religion and a number of philosophies, for that matter) are filled with potentially offensive claims that do not specifically concern this uniquely Christian doctrine.

Granting this distinction, let us first take a look at nonessential offense. In Matthew 15 Jesus' disciples report to him that his preaching has offended the Pharisees. Among the issues at hand is Jesus' claim that what goes into the mouth does not defile a person, but instead what comes out. The Pharisees are troubled by the disciples' shirking their duty to follow appropriate ceremonial regulations for washing their hands before eating. Jesus claims that the disciples did not defile themselves, but rather the Pharisees themselves were defiled—not by taking in something unclean or in an unclean manner, but when they bore false testimony and slander. The offense at issue here concerns proper interpretation of the law, and thus Jesus offends because his interpretation of the law clashes with the Pharisees.' The offense in this passage is not directly tied to his status as God-human but occurs when he challenges the Pharisees' religiosity. This example of offense resembles the kinds of offense we find among the Hebrew prophets in the Old Testament. Dozens of God's spokesmen are persecuted and killed as a result of the message they deliver. It is no wonder, since their message usually concerns the people's wicked turning from God's path to their own. Nonessential offense is thus a broad category and occurs any time one challenges the moral assumptions of an individual, group or society, as when Martin Luther King Jr. fought the racial injustice of his day.

Even though King was a Christian and even though he would describe his fight as rooted in his Christian faith, what offended those who disagreed with his message did not concern the specific doctrine of Christ. There-fore to call this category of offense nonessential is neither to criticize it nor to suggest it is not part of the Christian witness. Rather, in making the distinction Kierkegaard means to (1) differentiate it from offense at the person of Christ himself and (2) qualify its usefulness for the Christian witness. For the most part nonessential offense concerns morality, whereas essential offense concerns a particular theological doctrine. Thus non-essential offense *not* in the service of essential offense can end up being little more than moralism if it does not serve the gospel. It can lack the grace that follows essential offense, the grace that is central to the message of God Incarnate.

Perhaps the most useful and biblically warranted form of nonessential offense pertinent to Christian witness is the proclamation of Christian-ity's *bad news* prior to its proclamation of the *good news*. Of course I'm referring to the Christian doctrine of sin. It is hard to conceive how con-veying the doctrine of sin would not offend, given its meaning and im-plications. But this leads us full circle to a point that's been established— that the communication of Christianity is primarily through existence. In other words, while there's no getting around the fact that the doctrine of sin will offend, there might be a gentler way. We must not forget that one can communicate this doctrine existentially—through contrition and shared reflection on one's own sin with others. When a Christian's witness includes humility, repentance and forgiveness the doctrine of sin can be conveyed in a potentially compelling way.

Essential (theological) offense. Luke 5 records another story of Jesus offending the Pharisees. A group of men deliver their friend, a paralytic, to Jesus to be healed. Impressed by the faith of the friends, who go so far as to lower the paralytic through the roof of the home, Jesus responds, "Friend, your sins are forgiven you." Luke records the response of the Pharisees as follows: "Then the scribes and the Pharisees began to question, 'Who is this who is speaking blasphemies? Who can forgive sins but God alone?'" (Lk 5:20-21). Here we have a clear picture of es-sential offense. The Pharisees are scandalized not by a moral challenge to their lives—that they are acting unjustly or unfaithfully—but by a human claiming to do something only God can do—forgive another person's sin. Their response illustrates both the seriousness of essential offense and how central to Christianity the doctrine of the incarnation is. The idea that God became human scandalizes the Pharisees' theology, so much so that they accuse Jesus of blasphemy. Importantly, essential offense can scandalize an atheist's theology as well.[5] Clearly some without any religious faith find the idea of a God incarnate to be fanciful, incoherent and thus irrational.

Kierkegaard specifies two kinds of essential offense, or offense at the person of Jesus Christ: first, offense at Jesus' *loftiness*, "that an individual human being claims to be God, acts or speaks in a manner that manifests God," and second, offense at God's *lowliness*, "that the one who is God is this lowly human being, suffering as a lowly human being" (PC 82). In the Luke passage the Pharisees are offended in the first way: by Jesus' loftiness. Who does this man think he is, they wonder, that he should presume himself to be God? Someone like that is either insane or blasphemous. Kierkegaard cites John 6 as another passage that offends in this way. Speaking to a crowd of people Jesus makes a number of claims that cause them to "grumble." "I am the bread of life. Whoever comes to me will never be hungry, and whoever believes in me will never be thirsty" (Jn 6:35). Then, "I am the living bread that came down from heaven. Whoever eats of this bread will live forever" (Jn 6:51). Offense at Jesus' loftiness is offense at a human claiming to be divine. To call such offense essential is to claim that if this offense is omitted from one's proclamation, one has not proclaimed the gospel of Jesus Christ.

Since the European Enlightenment, offense at the claim that Jesus is God incarnate has been manifest directly and indirectly in the critiques of Christian faith by a number of thinkers who have tried to explain the psychological and sociological roots of religious belief. Ludwig Feuerbach,

---

[5]Yes, an *atheist's theology*. At least in some minimal sense everyone has a theology insofar as one has some defined view of God. If an atheist constructs an argument against religious faith, he or she is arguing that God, conceived in some particular way, does not exist. That is, the atheist will be able to describe this being's attributes or what they take this concept of God to include. This is helpful for the Christian to recognize, since sometimes the "God" atheists seek to refute is not the "God" Christians worship, in which case the argument may fall short. For example, if someone constructs a powerful argument against God, but the God he or she proves does not exist is a divine Santa Claus who functions as a gift giver and disappears for the better part of the year, then it's not clear such an argument has threatened Christian belief.

the German philosopher, claimed essentially that theology is anthropology—that beliefs humans hold about God are really humans projecting their own ideals onto a made-up object that can handle the weight of those claims (a nonexistent entity). Thus when religious people talk about God they're really just talking about themselves, albeit in a roundabout and ignorant fashion. Where humans fail to live out their ideals successfully, Feuerbach says, God can perfectly fulfill them. In effect, Jesus (the human) commits this fallacy as dramatically as anyone else when he projects his own religious ideals in such a way that he claims he himself is that perfect, ideal being, God. For the rest of us who hold faith in Jesus, we unknowingly concede our own failures to live up to our ideals when we ascribe perfection not only to an otherworldly deity but one who comes to earth in the form a perfect human being. Feuerbach's argument, significantly influential on a number of important thinkers such as Marx and Freud, can be seen from a Kierkegaardian perspective as a variation on offensiveness at the loftiness of Jesus of Nazareth. Who is this human who claims to be God? Someone who—because of his own shortcomings and those of his clan—needs there to be a God and therefore takes on the role himself.

If Feuerbach's position expresses offense at the loftiness of Jesus, fellow German Friedrich Nietzsche, forty years Feuerbach's junior, seems offended by the lowliness of God in Christ. Nietzsche views the relinquishing of power and thus the valuing of Christian virtues like humility and meekness as utterly absurd. To Paul's claim "Whenever I am weak, then I am strong" (2 Cor 12:10), Nietzsche would reply, "Whenever you are weak, you are weak!" Strength acts according to its nature, which Nietzsche assumes to be domination: "To demand of strength, that it should *not* manifest itself as strength, that it should *not* be a will to overpower, to subdue, to become master of . . . is as absurd as to demand of weakness that it should manifest itself as strength."[6] As we have seen above, however, Christianity's conception of power is much different—it is indeed the giving up of power. Simone Weil, whose pointed responses to Nietzsche often go under the radar, goes so far as to describe the

---

[6]Friedrich Nietzsche, "Genealogy of Morals," in *Readings in the Philosophy of Religion*, 2nd ed., ed. K. J. Clark (Buffalo, NY: Broadview, 2008), 270.

litmus test of true religion as tied to what a deity does with power: "The religions which represent divinity as commanding wherever it has the power to do so seem false."[7] Kierkegaard and Weil believe that it is a greater demonstration of power *not* to act in a dominating fashion even though one could do so than it is to act in such a way almost by necessity. In effect, Nietzschean offense is offense at the idea of a God who would— in an act of power—relinquish that very power. Nietzsche is correct that we should not expect a lion *not* to devour a lamb, but whether his analogy applies to what we should expect of God is a different question. While Nietzsche's target is primarily religious people themselves, the doctrine of a God who became a servant of humans unquestionably represents a stumbling block for someone who maintains such a position.

Offense at Jesus' loftiness and offense at God's lowliness represent offense essential to Christianity itself, and thus they represent offense essential to the Christian witness. For this reason Kierkegaard argues that one must pass by the possibility of offense if he or she is to come to faith. There is no back-door route to faith that can look past or sweep under the rug the notion that a human claimed to be God, nor is there a back-door route that can ignore that the God of all the universe thought it a good idea to exchange that status for the status of a servant of mere mortals. To witness to a Jesus or a God in any other way is, to borrow from Feuerbach (and Freud), to witness to nothing more than one's own projection of Jesus and God.

PROBLEMS WITH APOLOGETICS

Essential offense is essential to the Christian witness. Kierkegaard writes, "A person's shadow does not accompany him more inseparably than the possibility of offense at the God-man, for the God-man is the object of faith" (PC 121). In claiming that Jesus the God-man is the object of faith, Kierkegaard means a few things. First, Jesus is the one in whom Christians place their trust, the one who came from God the Father and the one who saves humans from their sin. Kierkegaard also means, however, that as the object of faith, Jesus is *not* the object of human reason, *not* the

---

[7]Simone Weil, *Waiting for God*, trans. Emma Craufurd (New York: Harper, 2001), 89.

conclusion to some logical argument, *not* the answer to some proof. Thus in the next sentence he writes, "The God-man . . . exists *only* for faith" (PC 121, italics mine). Though Kierkegaard himself is a philosopher, though he writes dozens of books containing hundreds of arguments, though he values the life of the mind as much as anyone, he is highly critical of what has come to be known as apologetics—the attempt to defend faith using rational arguments or arguments that do not already assume the truth of Christian faith. A rational defense of faith is no substitute for a Christian's lived witness to the world.

Before looking further at Kierkegaard's position, let us provide some theological context. Christian theologians tend to break down the concept of revelation—that God reveals himself to humans—into two categories: general and special revelation. General revelation refers to knowledge of God accessible to all people at all times in all places. One of the clearest explanations of general revelation comes from Romans 1:20: "Ever since the creation of the world his eternal power and divine nature, invisible though they are, have been understood and seen through the things he has made. So they are without excuse." John Calvin explains general revelation using the idea of a *sensus divinitatis*, or divine sense, that he claims all people possess. These claims help to explain why when we study the history of human civilizations worldwide we find people group after people group that hold some set of religious beliefs or another. Though the knee-jerk attitude of Christians is often to caricature and condemn pagan religions, it is important first to realize that the very tendency for all people to hold some religious belief at all is itself a gift of God.

What sort of ideas could be known through general revelation? First, one might be able to discern there is a God. Second, one might be able to discern that the God holds great power, or at least more than the average person. Third, one might reason that the God controls humans' fate or destiny, and thus, fourth, one is obligated to conform to what this God decrees. Many Christian theologians have maintained that arguments can be generated to support basic claims such as these, and so, for example, Thomas Aquinas famously shows five ways one can prove God exists. While Thomas himself believes in the Christian God, the God that is the conclusion of his proofs is a generic conception of God that is compatible with Christian teaching but does not exhaust what Christians believe about God. While some have found Aquinas's five ways encouraging to their faith, Kierkegaard has little interest in developing such proofs because, like Calvin and like Paul (in Romans), he believes proofs are not necessary. Everyone *already* has some sense of some divinity out there—we don't need to construct arguments to legitimate that sense. He provokingly writes, "There [has] never been an atheist, even though there certainly have been many who have been unwilling to let what they know (that the god exists) get control over their minds" (JP 3:3606). If Kierkegaard is correct and if Paul is correct, then atheism is not a purely intellectual position, which means atheism cannot be overcome by purely intellectual tools such as proofs. Kierkegaard believes that the chief problem is the will and its desires, and here Christians can of course sympathize with atheists. Allowing God to "get control" over our minds would change everything about our lives—our habits, our goals, our relationships, our vocations and so on.[8]

Special revelation refers to the knowledge of God that God has revealed to a particular people in a particular place and at a particular time, and it is this very particularity that has at times offended those outside the Christian faith. Most of the time special revelation refers to the witness of the Bible, and theologians dating back to Aquinas himself have long claimed that special revelation can only be known through faith, while matters of general revelation can be known through reason or through observation. Essential Christian teachings, which we have now spent considerable time addressing, such as the incarnation, the doctrine of sin or the Trinity, are all viewed as specially revealed doctrines for which there are no proofs. Instead, God grants the gift of faith to those who would believe.

To summarize, Kierkegaard thinks that proving matters of general revelation is unnecessary, since everyone already possesses some vague

---

[8]C. Stephen Evans writes, "On Kierkegaard's view, religious faith has declined among intellectuals, not because they are so smart, but because their imaginations are so weak and their emotional lives are so impoverished." "Kierkegaard, Natural Theology, and the Existence of God," in *Kierkegaard and Christian Faith*, ed. Paul Martens and C. Stephen Evans (Waco, TX: Baylor University Press, 2016), 52.

knowledge of God as a sort of foundation for religious belief. Moreover, he believes that the way these rational arguments work frontloads them for belief or nonbelief. Borrowing a term from British philosopher of religion John Hick, Kierkegaard understands that the world can appear "religiously ambiguous"; the world can seem to have some divine creator sometimes, but then in other lights—say when awful evils occur—it can seem that no such creator exists. Because of this apparent ambiguity Kierkegaard thinks all people either bring their theism or atheism into the argument, and so attempts to prove a God will be convincing to a theist, not because they are fully convincing but because the theist already sees the world that way. And such proofs will be unconvincing to atheists, not because they are fully unconvincing but because the atheist already sees the world without God. So, then, what's the point? And with regard to special revelation, Kierkegaard likewise thinks rational argument is pointless for the same reason the great majority of church fathers and theologians have thought it pointless—one must rely on God's special revelation for precise Christian knowledge of God and the world.

It is not difficult to challenge Kierkegaard on some of these issues. First, we might claim that in fact there could be benefits of theistic arguments—that our own faith might be edified through reflection on reasoned arguments for God's existence. We might not look to those arguments for total or conclusive proofs but rather for support. It seems that at least for some skeptics, demonstrating that theists have thought through their faith in a way that shows commitment to truth seems faithful to Peter's exhortation: "Always be ready to make your defense to anyone who demands from you an accounting for the hope that is in you" (1 Pet 3:15). Second, concerning matters of special revelation, showing how the Christian story and its specific claims about Jesus, for example, speak to universal human needs in a meaningful and powerful way seems an important task for faithful Christians in a Western context that seems to grow more pluralistic each day. Consider C. S. Lewis's arguments in *Mere Christianity*. It would be a mistake to view his discussions of Jesus and the doctrine of sin as rational explanations or proofs of Christian truth, but on the other hand, what has made that book so valuable to so many is Lewis's sustained argument that Jesus is indeed the message from God that humans have been longing for, though they didn't know it. Therefore, Kierkegaard's aversion to the rational exploration of faith seems harsher than it needs to be.

What, then, can we take away from this discussion? First, faith in Jesus Christ is ultimately a gift of God (Eph 2:8-9), and thus in terms of Christian witness one must remember, "Unless the LORD builds the house, those who build it labor in vain" (Ps 127:1). The project of sharing Christian faith with others is God's project, though one in which he has invited our participation (2 Cor 5:18). Praying that God would grant others the eyes of faith is without question a more effective approach than bending over backwards to show faith's rationality. Second, though Kierkegaard might overstate the case against engaging in apologetics, we can nevertheless glean a valuable lesson. Without proper care apologetics can quickly descend into the intellectualization of faith, neglecting the fact that our movement toward God is partly intellectual but also related to the heart. As Augustine says, "Our *hearts* are restless till they rest in Thee."[9] Likewise Kierkegaard writes,

> The good news of the Gospel is not to be foisted on people by means of demonstrations and reasons, demeaningly, as when a mother must sit and beg her child to eat the good wholesome food, but he turns up his nose at it and does not really care to eat. No, the appetite has to be aroused in a different way—and then the glad news of the Gospel will certainly be found to be appetizing. (JFY 203)

Effective witness will avoid the anti-intellectual, to be sure, but it must engage the depths of human souls, and this is far more likely when human lives communicate the gospel through actions of love, through kindness to the undeserving, through unexpected generosity and through humble interaction with the unbelieving. Notice what Paul says in 2 Corinthians 5:14: "For the love of Christ urges us on." It is not Christ's rational explanation of the world or of God or of ourselves but his overwhelming love that grabs us and draws us to him.

As a final word about apologetics and offense, let us sum up by saying that Kierkegaard advocates that we be faithful to Scripture's claims about

---

[9]Augustine, *Confessions*, trans. F. J. Sheed (Indianapolis: Hackett, 2006), 3, emphasis mine.

offense through clearly showing that out of great love God became human and dwelt among us. When love is the mode of our communication—whether about Jesus or about the doctrine of sin—we are far more likely to imitate Christ in compelling others about the good news. To the topic of love we now turn.

QUESTIONS FOR REFLECTION

1. What words, ideas and doctrines do I find essential to my Christian witness? What actions?

2. How do I deal with the offensive claims of the gospel in my communication?

3. What are ways I might communicate the gospel without words?

5

THE LIFE OF CHRISTIAN LOVE

The ordinary kind of Christianity is: a secularized life, avoiding
major crimes more out of sagacity than for the sake of conscience,
ingeniously seeking the pleasures of life—and then once in a while
a so-called pious mood. This is Christianity—in the same sense
as a touch of nausea and a little stomachache are cholera.

FOR SELF-EXAMINATION, 202-3

I𝐅 YOU WERE TO SURVEY THE NONRELIGIOUS to ask them the reason for their views, you might expect to hear things like "Faith is irrational" or "How could anyone believe in God with so much evil in our world?" These sorts of responses reflect *intellectual* obstacles to faith, but one might also come across *institutional* obstacles, as in the case of those who describe themselves as "spiritual but not religious." People of this persuasion very often believe in God and affirm other religious-sounding ideas such as good deeds or karma, but they mistrust the idea of religious authority, whether in the form of a religious leader or a historical religious group. There may be a third, equally powerful motivation why some keep their distance from religious communities and institutions: *hypocrisy.* This obstacle's root is the all-too-common reality that religious people often fail to practice what they preach; they are hearers but not always doers of the word (Jas 1:22-25). More than a few self-identified atheists, agnostics and spiritual types reared in churches exited those churches on being burned by clergy or fellow parishioners, and so they would cite hypocrisy not only as a reason to turn from organized religion and/or God but as a source of deep pain and suffering. Perhaps, the reasoning goes, there is something fundamentally wrong with Christianity if it so frequently produces such hypocritical people. Whether or not that is true, it nevertheless seems that hypocrites make participation in a religious community more trouble than it's worth. The objection from hypocrisy is thus a deeply personal one, and yet it is also one that people of faith themselves should be able to understand.[1] Which churches, which Christians, does hypocrisy not touch?

Bearing in mind the weight of this concern, in the present chapter we continue and expand our discussion of Christian existence, keeping in mind questions addressed earlier. What does life look like for the self (discussed in chapter three) who has come into relationship with the truth, Jesus Christ (discussed in chapter two)? Kierkegaard's answer to this question can be located primarily in the two great commandments of Christ, "'You shall love the Lord your God with all your heart, and with all your soul, and with all your mind.' This is the greatest and first commandment. And a second is like it: 'You shall love your neighbor as yourself'" (Mt 22:37-39). Through *loving and faithful worship of God* and *loving actions toward others*—Kierkegaard calls them works of love—one fulfills God's law but also moves toward the self God created one to become. The lone way out of despair in which the self rests transparently in its Creator can now be described as *loving* trust in God. And the expression of the self's gratitude toward God is obedience to God's law to care for others who, like me, despair and who, like me, need to rest in God's embrace. Given these commands, and in concert with our examination in chapter four, it follows for Kierkegaard that the "essentially Christian . . . is not related to knowing but to acting" (WL 96). Loving worship of God and care for others understood this way both prevents and potentially disarms the objection from hypocrisy.

---

[1]The hypocrisy objection to religion could be the strongest of the three noted. There are strong, intellectually sound responses to be made to the issues of faith's irrationality and the problem of evil, as there are to the individualized spirituality position, but sometimes the only response to the hypocrisy objection is to agree with the objector and subsequently try to live a holy life.

Kierkegaard says much about the Christian life, but here our focus shall be on love, and the reasons for this are straightforward. Although Kierkegaard's thought about ethics is vast, he wrote one book devoted entirely to a single Christian ethical idea, *Works of Love*, so such a focus is a natural and helpful way to constrain the subject matter. Further, as we will see below, Kierkegaard explores other virtues of the Christian life such as faith and hope *through* the concept of love. Kierkegaard would likely agree with St. Thomas Aquinas's claim that love is the "mother of the virtues," that every Christian virtue is born of love. Third, and most important, Scripture (and church tradition, as in Thomas) presents love as *the* distinguishing feature of the Christian life, and Kierkegaard himself affirms the biblical witness to that end, calling it "the highest good" (WL 239). As cited above, the Great Commandment of Jesus is to love God and subsequently to love one's neighbor, and in 1 Corinthians Paul upholds the preeminence of love as "the greatest of these." John identifies God as *love* (1 Jn 4:8), and throughout the Old Testament a number of writers speak of God's steadfast love as among his most characteristic attributes (e.g. Ex 20:6; Lam 3:22; Ps 36; Is 63:7). At every moment in Kierkegaard's thorough investigation of love his thought is derived from Scripture, whether Matthew 22 or 1 Corinthians 8 or Romans 13 or 1 John 4. In short, looking at what Kierkegaard says about Christian love—while by no means a full picture of his ethical thought—meets our objective, which is not to become better Kierkegaard scholars but more faithful Christians.

One other factor commends our focus on love. Through the nearly four-hundred-page text of *Works of Love* Kierkegaard repeatedly makes the case that the concept of Christian neighbor love is radically unlike the world's (or the poets', or Hollywood's) conceptions of love. We might call this Kierkegaard's "uniqueness thesis" insofar as he believes (1) the Christian view of love is sui generis (one of a kind) and therefore (2) it could not arise in any human heart. The implication is that the very idea of Christian love, not to mention its embodiment in human lives, is of divine origin.[2] Whether or not this thesis is compelling as an argument

---

[2]Describing a virtue concept as "of divine origin" places Kierkegaard in line again with Aquinas, who claims that love (along with faith and hope, as we will see shortly) is a theological

does not concern us here, but I point this out to illustrate how distinctive Kierkegaard believes Christian existence ought to be by comparison with non-Christian existence. If Christian love is radically different from other conceptions of love, and if Christians are recognizable *by their love* for others (Jn 13:35), then one cannot overestimate the importance of prayerful reflection on love and spurring one another on toward works of love. Without love, Paul says, we are "nothing."

LOVE'S LOVE

There are different places within Scripture that one may find lists and definitions of virtuous traits of the Christian life. The Beatitudes of Matthew 5 and Luke 6 commend a number of things, not all of which are virtues; among these are purity of heart, meekness (or gentleness), poverty (spiritual in Matthew and literal in Luke) and peacemaking. In Galatians 5 Paul enumerates the fruit of the spirit, which includes some of the same, such as peace and gentleness, but also joy and self-control. There are passages of Scripture that go into depth about a particular trait, as when the writer of Hebrews historically elucidates faith's righteousness in Hebrews 11. Arguably the best-known New Testament passage focused on one virtue or fruit of the Christian life is Paul's eulogy of love in 1 Corinthians 13, read at more Christian weddings than not. Paul begins 1 Corinthians 13:13, "And now faith, hope, and love abide, these three." Throughout church history many theologians have interpreted Paul as suggesting that these three virtues stand above the rest, with some, like St. Thomas, referring to them exclusively as the three theological virtues. Though Kierkegaard does not use that language—in fact, he doesn't use "virtue" language much at all—faith and hope are given nearly equal attention in his authorship, including in *Works of Love* itself. Drawn from 1 Corinthians 13:7, two of the chapters of *Works of Love* (Kierkegaard calls them deliberations) are titled "Love *Believes* All Things—and Yet Is Never Deceived" and "Love *Hopes* All Things—and Yet Is Never Put to Shame"

---

virtue. Theological virtues have three traits: (1) they are made known or revealed by God (Kierkegaard's point here); (2) they are infused by God (we have them thanks to God's gifting, unlike regular virtues, which we develop through habit and hard work); and (3) their object is God. I have argued elsewhere that Kierkegaard would agree that faith, hope and love are each of these things.

(emphases mine). For Kierkegaard faith and hope are not ideas to be examined separately from love, but since they flow from love they must be studied in the light of love. Thus we will begin by looking at love's love—the unique concept of Christian neighbor love—and then move on to the faith love has and the hope love has. As a chapter primarily on Christian ethics, our attention will be on the second greatest commandment—loving the neighbor—and thus we will find that faith and hope, while rooted in faith in Christ Jesus and hope in the coming of his reign, pertain instead to the faith and hope one has in relation to one's neighbor. Following John's claim that "whoever does not love [the neighbor] does not know God" (1 Jn 4:8), Kierkegaard maintains that our relationships to God, to our neighbor and to ourselves are all messily and inextricably related. Insofar as there is trouble in one, there will be trouble for the others, and insofar as there is health in one, there will be health for the others. Put another way, the two great commandments cannot be divorced.

Command and duty. We began our discussion of the self in chapter three by looking at what follows from the facts that (1) God created humans and (2) he created them in his image. As created beings humans are inherently relational beings, and the ultimate fulfillment of human life can be found only in a restful relationship with God, who also redeems and sustains us. Redemption would not be necessary except that humans use their freedom to choose other things, themselves included, over God. Turning now to a second kind of outward relation—one's fellow humans—Kierkegaard believes with Scripture that the task of becoming the self God created one to become is impossible in a social vacuum. We were not created to be islands and so we cannot flourish in our own self-enclosed worlds. (The "real world" of the film *The Matrix*, in which humans develop alone inside their own individual capsule, is *not* the real world, thank God!) The process of *individual* human flourishing, a priority of contemporary Western culture, necessarily includes flourishing relationships with others: if I have not love, I have nothing. However, just as one naturally chooses oneself, a career and a variety of other goods over God, so too do we sometimes choose these things over others. In fact, oftentimes we use others solely as a means to attain these goods. Anyone who's been befriended but, it turns out, only for the purposes of a pyramid scheme knows the pain of being a means to someone's end. But neither careers nor the goods they produce bear the image of God. Because (1) God expects one to relate lovingly to others—all others are as much God's image-bearing creation as I am—*and* because (2) I do not naturally or joyfully love all others as God's image-bearing creations, (3) God must *command* me to love them.

Kierkegaard is probably right that the very idea of commanded love will strike those unfamiliar with the Judeo-Christian tradition as offensive. Love seems primarily to be an emotional concept concerned with feeling a certain positive way about someone. To be *commanded* to feel positively about someone—especially someone one is inclined to hate or to disregard—seems odd, perhaps unfair and maybe impossible. It is like discovering the person you have met at a party is a professional comedian and then unthinkingly requesting that this person be funny. It's a ridiculous request; one cannot just turn on the humor switch any more than one turns on the warm and fuzzy feeling switch. To *have to* love seems not to love at all. It seems that genuine love comes forth naturally, from the heart, not from a duty that is commanded. This objection is forceful but only on the surface, since it is only as strong as the concept of love it assumes. Christian love, according to Kierkegaard, does not fundamentally pertain to *feeling* certain ways about others but instead to "sheer action" (WL 98). While there is undoubtedly an emotional component of Christian love, the command of Christ is not first *to feel* a certain way with regard to one's neighbor but *to act* a certain way toward one's neighbor. Clearly actions can be the subject of commands whether or not one feels like following them.

One might still worry that being commanded to act lovingly seems to admit of a gap between one's actions and one's heart, that the person who shruggingly follows the command cannot possibly have integrity since his or her inclinations and actions don't match up. Kierkegaard believes (in the spirit of Aristotle) that by regularly treating others lovingly— that is, by obeying the command—the emotional side of love will eventually come alongside love's actions, so that loving as both action and emotion will become second nature and the consistency of one's motivations and actions will be possible. Christians have a word for this process: sanctification. Through obedience to God's commands, one becomes more holy, more like God himself. God, who is love, acts and feels lovingly toward his creation in a perfectly consistent way; God is not duplicitous.

Kierkegaard's conclusion to *Works of Love* puts a fascinating spin on the notion that neighbor love is commanded, suggesting that the command itself is only provisional and that in the life of the sanctified Christian integrity of one's heart and mind is present. Notice the shift in tone in 1 John 4:7 from *command* to *proposal*: "Beloved, *let us love* one another." For the sanctified Christian who less and less seeks his or her own gain over others' and whose character is more and more rooted in love, the *command* to love becomes unnecessary because the self's desires and will have been transformed. Children who receive gifts do not by nature say thank you because they do not naturally feel gratitude, but instead parents command them to say thank you. But as children grow older and absorb the truth behind the command into both their behavior and character, they develop gratitude that naturally seeks expression in a thank you that does not need to be commanded. So it is with love.

Preference and self-denial. By being commanded to love the neighbor, love becomes a duty, an obligation, which sheds further light on the distinctiveness and offensiveness of Christian love. Unlike the love of neighbor, all other forms of love are rooted in preference and inclination, and when through preference one naturally loves someone, then the talk of treating that person well because it is a duty seems absurd. You do not visit your best friend in the hospital because you feel you have to but because you want to. You do not take your beloved on a date because it is your obligation but because it is the desire of your heart.

Love for friends or a beloved emerges out of inclinations over which one has little initial choice, but in pursuing those one finds attractive one exercises choice by choosing some over others. Those one chooses are those one finds attractive in some way or another. Perhaps they are brunette, or perhaps they're into mountain biking. What Kierkegaard wants us to see is not simply that the other person is attractive but that he or she is attractive *to me*. What does this mean? Another offensive claim: "Christianity . . . knows what perhaps escapes the poets, that the love they celebrate is secretly self-love" (WL 19). "I like Brett because he, like *me*, enjoys mountain biking." What I like about Brett, Kierkegaard tells us, is something that either resembles *me* or gratifies *me* in some way. The hidden root of self-love in what appears to be innocuous, even noble, can be detected in Aristotle's definition of the friend as the "other I" (WL 53). Many of us would say that what draws us to some friend or lover and not others is that we like best who *we* are in their presence. So even though we like or love these others, much of what we find likable or lovable about them is the way they make us feel about ourselves. Kierkegaard does not outright condemn these loves but wishes to point out their self-directedness as a primary conceptual distinction from the kind of love Jesus commands.

If preferential love views the friend or beloved as the other I, Christian neighbor love understands the neighbor as the first you (WL 57). It follows that this kind of love will better respect and preserve others' dignity since it does not serve the end of making *me* happy or getting *me* something. Love that fails to view the other as the first you and fails to desire the dignity of the other is always in danger of a kind of narcissism that "wants everyone to be transformed in his image, to be trimmed according to his pattern for human beings" (WL 270). But neighbor love loves by virtue of who the neighbor is in relation to God. Christian love thus seems paradoxical: on the one hand one loves the neighbor *based on his or her similarity* to all others—being creations of a loving God. Yet on the other hand one loves the neighbor *in all of his or her uniqueness and differences*—distinct traits that need not suit me or my preferences. Neighbor love replaces self-love with self-denial, thereby allowing the neighbor to become the self he or she was created to become.[3] The one who loves in this way recognizes the distinctiveness of humans as "God's gift by which he gives being to me and . . . to all" (WL 271).

---

[3]When neighbor love sanctifies parental love, parents stop living vicariously through their children by trying to mold them into some self-fulfilling construct.

The middle term, eternal security and equality. Another way to describe preferential love is as follows:

I—preference—other I

So, for example,

Mark—literal neighbor, collection of shared experiences, love of good beer, allegiance to Baylor sports—Drew

The preferences listed between Drew and me are just a few of the things we share in common, things that bond us together and things around which we relate. And yet clearly these reasons why I *prefer* Drew to several other would-be friends can dissipate, erode. Suppose Drew moves to Portland, and suppose our shared experiences subsequently become few and far between. Suppose my physician orders me to stop consuming alcohol, or suppose I become disillusioned with collegiate athletics. Those preferences that held our relationship together—things that gave *me* satisfaction in relation to Drew—are no longer commonly held. My love for and friendship with Drew may wane. Or consider a romantic relationship:

Mark—collection of shared experiences, sexual attraction, children, wittiness and humor, honesty—Amy

Again, these middle terms that bond Amy and me are each subject to change in a variety of ways, and consequently I can come to *prefer* other would-be lovers to Amy when this happens. I can find what I have in common with others more gratifying. Kierkegaard's point is something we all already know: that preferential loves are fickle, always subject to change and erosion. Preferential loves are only as sure as each party's enduring commitment to the preferences one has for the other. While many if not most of these middle terms or preferences are goods and treasures to be enjoyed, they are nevertheless fading goods "where moth and rust consume" (Mt 6:19).[4]

Christian neighbor love does not eliminate the middle term but exchanges it for God. "Christianity teaches that love is a relationship

---

[4]Middle term is a concept of logic that relates two premises.

between: a person—God—a person" (WL 107). God mediates one's relation to others, so when one sees the neighbor one sees that neighbor *through* God, as an image-bearer of God. In his discussion of cities as places dear to God's heart, Tim Keller describes crowded New York subways as among the most beautiful places on earth since they contain so many image-bearers of God in so little space.[5] If we relate to others through God—that is, if our love for others is dependent on God's love for them—then clearly this sort of love is on surer footing than preferential forms of love. God as the middle term, we might say, is going nowhere, and neither is the other's kinship to God. This is particularly useful as we differentiate our neighbors as "Christian" or "Muslim" or "atheist" and so on. Regardless of the belief or lack of belief of our neighbors, they are related to God. Kierkegaard thus describes Christian love as eternally secured in that no matter how the neighbor changes, even if the neighbor comes to hate you, you can nevertheless hold steady in obedience to God's command to love since the commitment to do so finds its source not in one's inner strength or positive feelings for the other but in the strength and power of God. In fact, this may explain how one can simultaneously love someone—act toward them with care—and hate what that person does, as when parents struggle with the self-destructive behavior of their children. The roots of the parents' love run deep in the unconditionally secure love of God and therefore are far more capable of enabling love to endure painful circumstances. But even parent-child relationships fracture, and Kierkegaard believes that for any sort of preferential relationship—parent-child, friend-friend, lover-beloved—one ought first to relate to the other as neighbor, as one to whom one is fundamentally related through God. In this way, even when the preferences fade, even when a break has occurred, one nevertheless loves. Of course this will look differently for the friend who has moved away or the spouse with whom one shares a home. The point is something most Christians recognize—without God as the basis of any relationship it is one or two moments away from a painful fracture.

---

[5]Timothy Keller, "Should I Not Love That Great City?," sermon, Redeemer Presbyterian Church, New York, October 14, 2001.

In one of the oldest biblical texts Job relates to his own servants *through God* as the middle term:

> If I have rejected the cause of my male or female slaves,
>   when they brought a complaint against me;
> what will I do when God rises up?
>   When he makes an inquiry, what shall I answer him?
> Did not he who made me in the womb make them?
>   And did not one fashion us in the womb? (Job 31:13-15)

For Job, God's creation of all people serves as the basis of all humans' shared dignity and the basis for treating others as equals before the law. Recall from chapter two Kierkegaard's description of the king whose loving passion was unhappy because from all outward appearances of inequality he could not convey his love for the lowly maiden. The slave is the neighbor of Job, the lowly maiden is the neighbor of the king, not on the basis of similarity (read: preference) but on the basis of equality "before God, but unconditionally everyone has this equality and has it unconditionally" (WL 59).

Equality does not extend simply to one's status as an object of love but to the potential of all people to love others. The ability to love is not "an *excellence* of a few gifted individuals, similar to brains, literary talent, beauty, and the like." Instead, "every human being by his life, by his conduct, by his behavior in everyday affairs, by his association with his peers, by his words, his remarks" can love (WL 213). Our tally of offensive claims about Christian love grows. First, love is commanded. Second, Christian love requires one to love *all* people, even the unlovely ones. But, third, *all* people, even the criminal, the hateful, the mean-spirited and the self-deceived can potentially love me, love one another. For Kierkegaard, not only is there no place in Christianity for intellectual snobbery and arrogance—look at my degrees, at my income, at my career (recall the intellectual form of Pelagianism described in chapter two)— but there is no place for moral snobbery or moral arrogance. I am as near to hating my neighbor as the unlovely one is to loving his or hers. It is only by God's help that I can love the neighbor in the first place, and that gift is for *all*, not just for the righteous or the good or the churchgoing.

The cash value of this insight for Christian existence is to expand our imagination to construe all humans as potential co-lovers of all humans and of God. If I genuinely come to believe that even the unlovely can love me, then I am all the more likely to love them in the first place.

There is one further place equality extends: to the love of oneself. For some, *loving others* as their equals is a hard pill to swallow, but for others *loving themselves* as equals to others is the bigger challenge. Our culture's recent obsession with overcoming low self-esteem should make this clear. Kierkegaard is emphatic that the phrase *as yourself* not be downplayed or forgotten. Christian love does not eradicate self-love but clarifies what proper self-love looks like. If one loves the neighbor *as oneself* but one loves oneself the wrong way, then one fails to love either the neighbor or the self. For example, if I tend toward self-indulgence, then loving the neighbor *as myself* is not really love. Or if I tend toward self-deprecation, then loving the neighbor *as myself* is not really love. We saw above that loving the neighbor fundamentally involves helping the neighbor to love God, and the way to accomplish this is first to view the neighbor as God's image-bearing child. Similarly, proper self-love is, strange as it sounds, helping oneself to love God. This occurs when God becomes the middle term between me and myself, or when I relate to myself—my identity, personality, thoughts, goals—with God as a sort of filter. While this might sound bizarre, it is nothing less than David's method of self-reflection in Psalm 139:

> Search me, God, and know my heart;
> > test me and know my thoughts.
> See if there is any wicked way in me,
> > and lead me in the way everlasting. (Ps 139:23-24)

But it is also consistent with Kierkegaard's notion of the deep self described in the previous chapter. The practical consequence of Kierkegaard's depth psychology means that when I look at myself in the mirror, or when I contemplate my greatest achievements, or when I ponder my sin, or when I think of what's possible for me to accomplish, or when I consider the limits to my freedom, I ponder myself *through God* or with God in view. Christian neighbor love regards others as equal to me, but

I am equal to them as well, and this equality is checked by my love and worship of God, who has created me and all others in his image. To love myself through God is to recognize myself as a fallen child. Fallen connotes the effects of sin on every part of me, but child connotes my inheritance in Christ, the one relationship through which I can become the beautiful self God created me to become.

LOVE'S FAITH

The primary topic of chapter two was religious faith as it is ordinarily understood: faith in God or faith in Jesus Christ. Beliefs one holds about God naturally inform other beliefs, and Christian faith also has an ethical dimension that pertains specifically to what one believes to be true about the neighbor. Although love is "sheer action" and cannot be reduced to mere emotion, it is not action devoid of thought. There is a logic or rationality to Christian ethics, though this logic or rationality signifies a perspectival understanding and is internal to the Christian community. For those who rest in Christ as their redeemer and sustainer, the call to believe certain things about the neighbor makes all the sense in the world. But from a point of view outside faith, these beliefs can look absurd and irrational. Of course that does not mean they are false.

Love presupposes and calls forth love. Drawing on 1 Corinthians 8:1 Kierkegaard explores Paul's claim that "love builds up," which he states is love's "most characteristic specification" and one that is "exclusively characteristic of love" (WL 216, 212). Very quickly Kierkegaard points out that not everything that seems loving or upbuilding is that; most of us have done a seemingly noble deed that appeared loving and upbuilding but was little more than a means of trying to garner positive impressions from others. But it is also the case that something might *seem* unloving—the opposite of building up—and in fact be an act of love. In C. S. Lewis's *The Horse and His Boy* Aslan the lion chases after the protagonists, Shasta and Aravis, clawing the latter's back as she gallops her horse toward Narnia. Not knowing Aslan at the time, the youths are shocked into moving full steam ahead, and they count themselves lucky to have escaped the lion's attack with a mere flesh wound. Later, however, they discover the identity of the lion and recognize

Aslan's actions as directed toward their good—escaping the oncoming march of Prince Rabadash. Aslan points out that a pep talk would not have sufficed to encourage the party to speed up their journey, but fear alone would work to accomplish this end. Aslan's behavior appears unloving and destructive, but as the broader picture is unveiled, it can be seen instead as loving and upbuilding.

The issue at stake is one of perspective, not just what one sees but how one sees it. Making much of the metaphorical language of construction in the predicate *builds up*, Kierkegaard notes the importance to a building of its foundation, and yet characteristic of a foundation is its invisibility. In the case of a house, one cannot know with certainty how well or poorly the house is built based on how it looks from the outside or even from the rooms inside. The house with a worn-out roof and peeling paint might have a stronger foundation and more years in front of it than the newly constructed house whose exterior looks perfect. Either way, making a judgment about the house involves faith about the foundation. Commanded love, likewise, involves faith about the foundation (or ground) of one's neighbor—who the neighbor really is in a most basic or fundamental sense. Our assessment of others usually goes no further than how they look to us—their appearance or behaviors. But we tend to recognize such evaluation as fairly shallow or at least incomplete. First impressions are often mistaken, and few of us have escaped behaving embarrassingly toward others when those impressions were without sure foundation or grounding (e.g., "When is your due date?" to the woman who is not pregnant).

So what is the foundation or ground of the neighbor? Kierkegaard's answer is unsurprising: "It is love. Love is the source of everything and, in the spiritual sense, love is the deepest ground of the spiritual life" (WL 215). This ethic is consistent with Kierkegaard's theology, since love as the ground implies God and God's loving act of creation. Kierkegaard offers a few illustrations to tease out love's unique vision. He speaks of a mother's love for her baby who falls asleep: "Just to see the baby sleeping is a friendly, benevolent, soothing sight, but it is not the upbuilding. If you still want to call it upbuilding, it is because you see love present, it is because you see God's love encompass the baby" (WL 214). In other words, love builds up by believing in a reality that is not directly evident. It is evident that the baby resting is a soothing sight, but it is not evident that in some way this picture reflects God's foundational love. God's creation of all things, including all humans, is a proposition of faith, not something observed. Likewise, to see in others—especially in far less lovely sights—that God is the foundation is itself a claim of faith.

This faithfulness in construing others not just as gentle sights or ugly sights or beautiful sights or terrifying sights but instead as God's loving productions—something one cannot see—is a central action or work of love. Love's faith sees others as God's: "See what love the Father has given us, that we should be called children of God" (1 Jn 3:1). Kierkegaard refers to love's faith as a *presupposition*, a belief that one brings to one's interaction with the neighbor, as opposed to a belief only affirmed *after* interaction with the neighbor has verified its truth. He writes, "*The one who loves presupposes that love is in the other person's heart*" (WL 216, emphasis original). Although outward appearances—actions, attitudes, words—may suggest otherwise, Christian love *believes* that love is nevertheless present even if it is subterranean. Without question love that presupposes love in the heart of another will appear irrational, since such a belief seems contrary to fact. However, its epistemic foundation—the intellectual support one has for this belief—rests in a belief Christians likely have far more confidence in, that God has created all people and done so with and through love.

When one presupposes love is present in another's heart, whether or not that love is evident, "*by this very presupposition* [one] *builds up love in him*" (WL 216-17, emphasis original). Not only is it loving to assume love is at the core of the neighbor, but this very assumption itself works to bring about love in the other. Love "loves forth" or love calls forth love, draws it out of the other (WL 217). When someone is loved, he or she is spurred on toward love. It is as though there is a magnetic attraction between love and love, what Kierkegaard calls the "like for like." The notion of love calling or drawing forth love seems analogous to the principle of Proverbs 15:1, "A soft answer turns away wrath, but a harsh word stirs up anger." Gentleness, especially when it is unexpected, often leads to a response of gentleness. Of course the inverse is true as well—hateful action breeds hateful action.[6] Love "draws out the good," because love demonstrates the truth of the neighbor's belief that love is present in the foundation of who they are (WL 217).

Love believes all things. The claim that love presupposes love in the other and in doing so calls forth love may strike one as interesting and even inspiring, but it is also irritating in that it seems practically false. Surely some of those we come in contact with lack any modicum of love whatsoever and loving treatment of them does *not* draw forth love but rather envy or entitlement or embarrassment. The presupposition that love is present in the heart of *all* people seems naive if not false. To believe such a claim seems to play into the hands of those critics who accuse the religious of wishful thinking. In "Love Believes All Things— and Yet Is Never Deceived" Kierkegaard seems aware of this objection, but surprisingly it does not seem to bother him, and instead he pushes the point even further. Drawing on Paul's claim in 1 Corinthians 13:7 that "love believes all things," Kierkegaard wishes to expose our defensive posture toward being deceived as a kind of prejudice whose root is mistrust—a lack of faith—and "a preference for evil" (WL 233).

The thread of love's faith or love's presupposition appears as early as the first page of the first discourse of *Works of Love*. "We can be deceived by believing what is untrue, but we certainly are also deceived by not believing what is true" (WL 5). Kierkegaard contends that the majority of humans operate with a kind of worldly wisdom or shrewdness that takes seriously the first concern but cares little for the second. They calculate their life's decisions, including interactions with and treatment of others, with an eye toward avoiding mistakes in judgment, giving less thought to the ways they might miss out on some good if they refrain from action. One might delay pursuing a friendship with a new coworker, or one might put off a marriage proposal, until one can be certain that these important decisions are more or less guaranteed to work out. To be sure, in contrasting these two ways Kierkegaard does not condemn patience or prudent deliberation, but instead he aims to draw a clear distinction between two kinds of wisdom one finds in the world and in the

---

[6]The related phrase "hurt people hurt people," while pithy, seems all too true from the perspective of my wife, who previously worked as an advocate for sexual assault victims.

kingdom of God. The problems with worldly wisdom are as follows: (1) it potentially closes one off to a certain kind of relational goods, and yet (2) it considers this strategy alone to be wisdom. Psychologist and philosopher William James describes such wisdom as the preference of error-avoidance to truth-acquisition. James believes that there is no rational basis to prioritize the former over the latter, since very often the former is rooted in fearful prejudices.[7] Godly wisdom recognizes that one can be wrong in more ways than one, including overdosing on worldly wisdom. One can try so hard to avoid being in error that the possibility of gaining truth is lost. Applied concretely to human relationships, godly wisdom recognizes that if one waits until one has sufficient evidence to invest in the life of one's neighbor, one will likely wait a long time (if not indefinitely) and consequently be closed off to all sorts of blessings the relationship might produce. Godly wisdom leans on truths about God and God's creation of humankind and thus is open to truthful relationships with others that worldly wisdom would resist.

There are two broad ways that neighbor love expresses faith or trust in the other when worldly wisdom would call such behavior foolish, wishful thinking. The first pertains to situations in which actions seem to reflect the opposite of love, when in reality they are actions of love. I noted above the story of Aslan chasing down Aravis and Shasta ultimately to save their lives. The second way love expresses trust in a manner offensive to worldly wisdom is a far more challenging pill to swallow, and this is when neighbor love maintains that love is present in the hearts of those we would describe as truly evil, hateful or malicious. Serial killers and rapists, terrorists and torturers come to mind. But lest we get lost in outliers, most of us likely find presupposing love remarkably difficult in the self-serving narcissist, the annoying know-it-all, the bigot, the gossip or the philanderer. Presupposing love in these types of people seems straightforwardly foolish both in that it seems like a false belief to have and a dangerous belief to act on. It seems that presupposing love in these sorts could expose one to real harm, whether emotional or social or in some cases physical.

---

[7]See James's famous essay "The Will to Believe."

Let us take the proverbial coworker who strikes us as a self-serving gossip who feigns humility but really is a narcissist who has gone and will go to nearly any length to gain a promotion. Kierkegaard wishes to distinguish between the knowledge we have of this person and what the knowledge implies about how they should be treated. We might ask ourselves what follows from the facts that this coworker has back-stabbed a friend, has made up stories about someone else to move up the ranks. It is normal to conclude that what follows is a justified kind of *essentializing* of this person. This person gossips, so he is a gossip. This person lies, so he is a liar, and so on. These behaviors express who this person fundamentally is, and therefore how he should be treated: as a gossip, as a liar. But Kierkegaard claims this does not follow at all. Or to speak more precisely, it may follow but not necessarily so. Knowledge of this coworker, we might say, is neutral. Where one goes with it—how one responds *in action* in one's relationship to this person— can go two directions. Worldly wisdom, with its fear of being deceived and duped, *mistrusts* the coworker for obvious reasons. It does not wish to be the next victim. But neighbor love does something different with this knowledge. Rather than essentializing the person and saying "this is who you really are," love "believes all things." But what does this mean? To believe all things makes little sense, at first glance, and sounds contradictory. In the light of our previous discussion, to believe all things is simply to believe that love is always present at the core of this individual even when it seems that such love is humanly impossible to locate. Love *believes* this not based on the knowledge of this person's bad behavior (obviously) but on the basis that God has created all people in his image with love as their foundation.

Clearly the ways mistrust and love treat the coworker will vary widely. Mistrust will keep distance to avoid being deceived or, if mis-trust engages with the coworker, it may even be strategic, making use of the coworker's tendencies toward slander or self-promotion. Mis-trust will *not* hold out anything in the way of serious hope or optimism for this person's reform, and for that reason mistrust will not view this person as someone he or she can help transform or someone with whom he or she can grow in friendship. Mistrust certainly does not recognize an obligation to steer the coworker toward the good (i.e., love the coworker). Love, on the other hand, will act based on trust, but note—not trust in the person's ability to self-transform but in God's ability to draw to the surface the deep seed of love. Love's actions will stand distinct from mistrust's actions, which over time will be clear to the coworker, who may notice mistrust's withdrawal and love's engagement. But love will also act to draw the better qualities out of the coworker because love believes love is present in the heart of the coworker, and this act of presupposing love calls forth or draws out that love. It is important to note that love's actions (like mistrust's actions) are not failsafe, and that the coworker may be unmoved by love. Love does not magically override human freedom. But does that mean that love believed all things and *was* deceived? Kierkegaard rejects this conclusion and claims that only mistrust can be deceived because mistrust fails to believe what is most true about any human—that love is present in the foundation of each created self. So, Kierkegaard claims, even if love seems duped or deceived, even if love is taken advantage of by the coworker, it is not difficult to see that the coworker is the one who is ultimately deceived, not love, because the coworker utterly lacks self-knowledge, whereas love knows the coworker better than he knows himself. Love knows the coworker is a child of God, made in God's image. It is not difficult to notice the utter consistency of Kierkegaard's biblical love ethic with his theology of creation, described in chapter three, a consistency that, if applied to Christians' lives, would turn the world upside down.

The idea that love believes all things also does not imply that love naively puts itself in all manner of dangerous situations for the sake of calling forth love in the other. One does not seek out dangerous alleys late at night to practice presupposing love in the other. Recall that love is related to a godly kind of wisdom, and thus it is not foolish. Nevertheless, there is inherent risk in loving this way. It is possible that when love engages the coworker, the coworker will not be moved (or moved immediately) but will respond with apathy or with suspicion or scorn. Such possibilities are inevitable. While love's engagement might therefore appear silly to some or hopeless to others, it primarily offends in its unyielding commitment to the belief that for God all things are possible, including the conversion of the most evil person. For this reason love's faith cannot be separated from love's hope that God will bring such conversion about.

LOVE'S HOPE

Just as the claim that "love hopes all things" follows the claim that "love believes all things" in 1 Corinthians 13:7, so too does Kierkegaard's exploration of love's hope follow the exploration of love's faith. This makes conceptual sense since hope that love will come forth is only possible if one has faith that love is present in the heart of the neighbor in the first place. If love's faith is lacking, then whatever hope can be conjured will be groundless and will indeed be wishful thinking. The assistance humans need to become whole in love can be found only supernaturally— through God. Much of the apathy we express toward those we would describe as hopeless can be tied back to a failure of faith in the truth that these creatures bear God's image as I do or as Job's servants do.

To hope all things is to hope always, but hope specifically concerns the future, which Kierkegaard calls a "duality." There are two ways the future can go—toward the good or toward evil. This open-endedness of the future becomes the basis for Kierkegaard's respective definitions of hope and fear. "To relate oneself expectantly to the possibility of the good is to *hope*, which for that very reason cannot be any temporal expectancy but is an eternal hope. To relate oneself expectantly to the possibility of evil is to *fear*" (WL 249). What usually goes by the name of hope is often just "a wish, a longing, a longing expectation now of one thing, now of another"; these "hopes" concern trivial contingencies of our temporal lives and often reflect our changing preferences (WL 250). I hope for a better job, a bigger house, more free time and so on. To hope in love's sense is not to leave to the side temporal desires but to view those desires in the light of eternity and the confidence one has in God's sovereign reign over all things, including the future. Thus hope is a relentless expectancy that the good will come to pass even when the odds suggest otherwise. And it's not simply that the good will come to pass but that because of God the good *can* come to pass.

Although Scripture often links old age to wisdom, when the elderly lack hope it offers a stark and instructive illustration of life without Christian love. The following quotation captures the degree to which a lack of hope is directly tied to the forms of despair described in chapter three. This person's life is

> a dull repetition and paraphrasing of the same old thing; no possibility awakeningly frightens; no possibility rejuvenatingly enlivens. Hope becomes something that belongs nowhere, and possibility something just as rare as green in winter. Without the eternal, one lives with the help of habit, sagacity, aping, experience, custom, and usage. Indeed, take all this, put it all together, cook it over the slow or the merely earthly blazing fire of passions, and you will see that you will get all kinds of things out of it, a variously concocted tough slime that is called practical sagacity. (WL 251)

This portrait of hope's absence is depressing and grotesque and demonstrates how literally impossible it would be for the one without hope to love the neighbor. If one relates to others merely out of habit and custom, and if the eternal is not in view but only the remaining futile years of temporal existence, then hoping the good for others and for oneself is out of the question. The denial of hope through the denial of the eternal implies that for this person "God's plan for existence is rejected" (WL 251).

While it might be easy to spot the elderly curmudgeon described above, the question Kierkegaard poses is to what extent do *I* lack love's hope, and if I do, how can I tell? The varieties of hopelessness are as varied as the varieties of despair, and so in asking this question it may be instructive to return to chapter three's discussion of the self as despairing in multiple ways. In the present deliberation of *Works of Love* Kierkegaard draws attention to two specific forms of hopelessness. On the one hand there is what I would call the "victim of life" character who lacks hope because, to recall Albert Camus's *Myth of Sisyphus*, this person has been undermined by life. He has been drained, spent, gobbled up and spit out. He "gives up possibility." The second form of hopelessness might be understood through the *Saturday Night Live* character Debbie Downer. This individual "is brazenly so bold as to *assume* the impossibility of the good" (WL 253). This is the person who presupposes almost anything but

love; she presupposes failure or error or futility. Both cases of hopelessness can be tied to how one relates to one's neighbor. The first form
of hopelessness does not engage the neighbor in love because such efforts
have failed before; or because out of guilt of her own failure she does not
believe the good can come for the neighbor; or simply because she is
fatigued to such an extent that the energy involved in hoping the good
for one's neighbor is too difficult to muster. The second, Debbie Downer–
form of hopelessness might, like mistrust, essentialize the neighbor, believing the neighbor incapable of love because "this is who he is." We
sometimes refer to this treatment as being boxed in, and most of us can
relate to the frustration and pain we feel when we are the object of such
hopeless treatment. Behind both forms of hopelessness it is often the
case that one's hopeless treatment of the other reflects hopeless treatment
of the self, so once again it is clear that how one loves others is bound to
how one loves the self and loves God.

Love's hope, by contrast, "continually holds possibility open with an
infinite partiality for the possibility of the good. That is, [the one who
loves in this way] lovingly hopes that at every moment there is possibility,
the possibility of the good for the other person" (WL 253). Kierkegaard
stages a conversation between despair (our Debbie Downer character)
and hope reminiscent of the earlier claim that faith has no less knowledge
to work with than mistrust. Despair looks at things and remarks,

> It is possible that even the most sincere enthusiast would at some time
> become weary, . . . that even the most fervent believer would at some time
> give up faith, . . . that even the most burning love would at some time cool
> off and freeze, . . . that even the best friend could be changed into an
> enemy, . . . therefore despair, give up hope, above all do not hope in any
> human being or for any human being. (WL 254)

Without justification despair claims that because bad things could
happen, one ought to bet that they will happen—that is the implication
of the "therefore" above. While despair would admit it's not a prophet, its
worldly wisdom dictates that in relation to what one expects about others
one ought to play things safe. Despair moves the self all the more inward,
in terms of emotional care for the neighbor but also in terms of how one

treats the neighbor. But the "therefore" in the quote above does not follow logically, and hope concludes a "therefore" of its own, the basis of which is love:

> Therefore never unlovingly give up on any human being. . . . Since it is possible that even the most prodigal son could still be saved, that even the most embittered enemy—alas, he who was your friend—it is still possible that he could again become your friend. It is possible that the one who sank the deepest—alas, because he stood so high—it is still possible that he could again be raised up. . . . Therefore never give up on any human being; do not despair, not even at the last moment—no, hope all things. (WL 254)

Two radically different orientations are possible, but we might ask whether hope is on any more solid footing than despair. From the view of despair, hope seems little more than wishful thinking and pipe dreams, whereas despair seems more true to past facts.

A few responses are in order. First, philosophers dating at least as far back as David Hume will warn us that the past is no guarantor of the future, so while we may have reason to think the sun will rise again tomorrow, to act as though it *must* happen is to mistake likelihood for necessity. For despair this means that deriving support from what has happened before is more anecdotal than evidential. This means, second, that to a great extent whether one despairs or hopes is a function of one's choosing.[8] That is, no appeal to reason leads to a despairing orientation rather than a hopeful one, no matter how much despair name calls hope as irrational. Third, how one chooses is revelatory—it tells us something deep about ourselves. As the case with faith versus mistrust, to choose hope over despair *reveals* love rather than mistrust or doubt as the motivator. Lest Kierkegaard be accused of suggesting that it is our hope that grounds our confidence in good possibilities that may come about, he clarifies, "Paul does not say that hope hopes all things but that love hopes

---

[8]Cf. "Everything has two handles, the one by which it may be carried, the other by which it cannot. If your brother acts unjustly, don't lay hold on the action by the handle of his injustice, for by that it cannot be carried; but by the opposite, that he is your brother, that he was brought up with you; and thus you will lay hold on it, as it is to be carried" (*Enchiridion* 43). These are the words of the great Stoic philosopher Epictetus, who likewise situates our treatment of others as a function of choice. One can see a faint glimmer of the Christian ethic of love.

all things" (WL 259). In other words, the basis of hope is love and love's presuppositions about others, their relation to God and God's power to do all things. Hope does not originate hope in some positive-thinking, mantra-repeating concentration of heart and mind. Hope comes from love, and love's hope has the confidence of love's faith since it is rooted in the actions and power of a loving God. The biblical basis for this hope can be seen in Jesus' claims about a rich man entering the kingdom of heaven. Noting that this event is less likely than a camel passing through the eye of the needle, Jesus nevertheless expresses that hope is not lost for the rich man since "for God all things are possible" (Mt 19:26). In these lights, from a Christian perspective of love, hope rather than despair seems more than justified. In fact, Christians who lack hope for others are in disobedience to the command to love: to lack hope for another, "to give up on him is to give up your love for him" (WL 255). By contrast, when one has hope in relation to one's neighbor, one "brings the best gift ever" since hope is rooted in the possibility of the good with "eternity's help" (WL 259).

Arguably the most poignant illustration of Christian hope can be found in the story of the prodigal son, in which the younger of two sons requests his inheritance of his father and leaves home only to squander it and return with nothing. Most often the story is read as an allegory in which the father represents God, who forgives the sins of the younger (and older) brother. But Kierkegaard reads the story as one of God's hope for his children and, subsequently, a model for the Christian's hope for her fellow human beings. Kierkegaard writes, "The prodigal son's father was perhaps the only one who did not know that he had a prodigal son, because the father's love hoped all things. . . . But love builds up, and the father won back the prodigal son simply because he, who hoped all things, presupposed that love was present in the ground" (WL 221).

To have love's faith that presupposes love in the neighbor and love's hope that for God all things are possible are among the high demands of Christian existence that Kierkegaard refers to as sheer action. One may wonder whether Kierkegaard enumerates specifically loving actions (like mowing your neighbor's lawn or cooking dinner for someone who is ill), but for the most part he avoids such specificity since he firmly believes that no action is of itself a loving action since it can be done for unloving reasons. Love's actions or the *works of love* are not add-ons, extra homework to do to make God happy, but rather they are the very ways by which humans realize their own identity and destiny before God. Just as God loves, so God's image-bearers are designed to love, and the payoff is simultaneously a restful relation in God and transformed relationships to others. To return to the obstacle of hypocrisy described at the outset of the chapter, my contention is that the best way to counter the argument itself and, more importantly, the pain and distaste caused by hypocrites, is not primarily through argument but through love and its variety of works.

QUESTIONS FOR REFLECTION

1. Describe the challenge of presupposing love in the neighbor. Do I have difficulty seeing the connection between my understanding of creation and the love ethic?

2. How does Christian hope avoid mere wish fulfillment?

3. Do I view love as a choice or something beyond my control? In what ways can I grow or develop in love?

CONCLUSION

LET US CONCLUDE BY RAISING A QUESTION that would likely occur to someone picking up this book for the very first time: What does it mean to be a *Christian* missionary to *Christians*? Is this even a coherent idea? We have seen why Kierkegaard believes such a task is not just possible but necessary.

- If there are some who are Christians in name only, then one can be a Christian missionary to such Christians.

- If there are some who have inherited a perverted form of Christianity and know nothing better, then one can be a Christian missionary to such Christians.

- If there are Christians who value created goods over the Creator, then one can be a Christian missionary to such Christians.

- If there are Christians who struggle to trust in God and his goodness, then one can be a Christian missionary to such Christians.

- If there are Christians who fail to believe God can redeem even the least redeemable person, then one can be a Christian missionary to such Christians.

- If there are Christians who lose hope that God's kindness, forgiveness and redemption extend even to them, then one can be a Christian missionary to such Christians.

- If there are Christians who "speak in tongues of angels," and so on, but have not love, then one can be a Christian missionary to such Christians.

Thus to be a missionary is not simply to convert the lost but to incarnate divine love in obedience to and imitation of Jesus Christ, the God incarnate. This could involve a fresh gospel message, works of love, words of nurture or the trust of one who construes me as a *neighbor* who bears God's image. The truth is that just as all Christians are called to mission, so too could *all* Christians use the message and love of the Christian missionary. Mission work quite simply calls others, *all* others, to God.

Kierkegaard's own call to his contemporaries, his message that extends even to us today, and his exhortation to Christians to love everyone they see can be described using one of his own favorite terms as a call to *earnestness*. A rich and ubiquitous concept throughout his works, it means the following things. First, earnestness connotes integrity, or the interconnectedness of our Christian beliefs with each aspect of our lives. I have touched on this topic in nearly every chapter of the book. The Christian's faith must match up with the Christian's actions, which must match up with the Christian's cares and concerns, motivations and desires, and so on. Earnest Christianity is comprehensive and internally cohesive—it is the sort of Christianity that, offensive or not, can *not* be accused of hypocrisy.

Second, earnestness for Kierkegaard means honesty before God. Though it might seem troubling, Kierkegaard's initial aim is not that the reader who finds his books should become Christian as much as it is that each person should finally become honest with God, themselves and the world, and then go on from there. It is for this reason that Kierkegaard suggests that a pagan who worships a false God with purity of heart and deep passion might be closer to the truth than the nominal Christian who identifies as Christian though has no real love, felt need or deep passion for God, whose worship is mere gesture. Whether Kierkegaard is right, the point he wishes to make remains a valuable challenge for every reader of this book. All of us know that if God exists, then God—as King David writes—searches our inmost parts. Yet how easily can one forget this, how quickly can one jump into patterns and habits of religiosity and quite literally lose heart, lose one's love for God and live dishonest lives that mimic more than practice the faith we claim.

Honesty before God and the coherence of each aspect of our lives are lifelong pursuits we will inevitably botch. Kierkegaard's exhortation to fellow Christians is a demanding call, a frustrating word that seeks to rouse, prick and prod us. It is no wonder why David Swenson labeled him the Danish Socrates; Socrates was the gadfly of Athens, a presence constantly stirring trouble among her citizens. Kierkegaard was Denmark's gadfly, though if we are lucky he can be ours, too. And should we struggle in the quest for Christian earnestness, should we sometimes fail in the mission God has given us all, I am thankful that we also find in Kierkegaard near-constant reminder of the gospel—that God's love and grace come free to us.

Suggestions for Further Reading

Primary Sources

A partial list of Kierkegaard's writings appears in the abbreviations at the front of the book. A number of his works may suit Christians as devotional readings, albeit more challenging than the average devotional reading. These include the following: *Christian Discourses, Eighteen Upbuilding Discourses, Upbuilding Discourses in Various Spirits* and *Discourses at the Communion on Fridays*. Translated by Sylvia Walsh. Bloomington, IN: Indiana University Press, 2011.

Kierkegaard's most important book on Christian ethics is *Works of Love*. The companion volume *For Self-Examination/Judge for Yourself!* offers fairly accessible essays that take as a point of their departure a variety of Scripture passages. *Practice in Christianity*, heavily drawn from in this book, also contains much rich insight for Christian living. For those interested in Kierkegaard's psychological thought, *The Sickness unto Death* is a challenging though rewarding read. For the philosophically inclined, I recommend *Philosophical Fragments* and Kierkegaard's most famous book, *Fear and Trembling*. These last three, however, are very challenging to those without a background in philosophy, so I strongly recommend reading introductory or supplemental essays.

When people ask me where to start in Kierkegaard, I actually recommend none of these initially but instead Charles Moore's excellent collection of passages and quotes from Kierkegaard called *Provocations: The Spiritual Writings of Kierkegaard*. Walden, NY: Plough Publishing

House, 2014. This is a highly accessible volume, and the readings are arranged thematically. This book also has the advantage of introducing new readers to Kierkegaard in such a way that they can find what interests them and then seek out the book from which particular passages are drawn.

SECONDARY SOURCES

For those who wish to learn more about Kierkegaard or particular aspects of his thought, I recommend the following:

Evans, C. Stephen. *Faith Beyond Reason: A Kierkegaardian Account.* Grand Rapids: Eerdmans, 1998.

———. *Kierkegaard: An Introduction.* Cambridge: Cambridge University Press, 2009.

———. *Kierkegaard's Ethic of Love: Divine Commands and Moral Obligations.* Oxford: Oxford University Press, 2004.

———. *Søren Kierkegaard's Christian Psychology: Insight for Counseling and Pastoral Care.* Vancouver, BC: Regent College Publishing, 1990 .

Gouwens, David. *Kierkegaard as Religious Thinker.* New York: Cambridge University Press, 1996.

Hall, Amy Laura. *Kierkegaard and the Treachery of Love.* New York: Cambridge University Press, 2002.

Rae, Murray. *Kierkegaard and Theology.* Edinburgh: T&T Clark, 2010.

Roberts, Robert C. *Faith, Reason, and History: Rethinking Kierkegaard's Philosophical Fragments.* Macon, GA: Mercer University Press, 1986.

Walsh, Sylvia. *Kierkegaard: Thinking Christianly in an Existential Mode.* Oxford: Oxford University Press, 2009.

Westphal, Merold. *Kierkegaard's Concept of Faith.* Grand Rapids: Eerdmans, 2014.

———. *Kierkegaard's Critique of Reason and Society.* Macon, GA: Mercer University Press, 1987.

Subject Index

Abraham, 45-46, 55, 115
aesthetic, 50, 52, 58-59, 101-10, 113
anxiety, 72, 90-97
apologetics, 63, 128-33
argument from Christendom, 67-68, 119
Aristotle, 63, 84, 140, 142
atheism, atheist, 37, 39, 48, 55, 57, 99-100, 126,
    130-31, 135, 144
attack upon Christendom, 30
Augustine of Hippo, Saint, 33-34, 44, 88, 90-91,
    93, 132
authority, 55, 86, 90, 135
autonomy, 63-64, 86, 92, 96, 108
Barth, Karl, 43
Bible, 32, 42, 45, 58, 60, 88, 118-19, 123, 139, 155
    New Testament, 30, 56, 61, 118, 124
    Old Testament, 52, 124, 137
Bono. *See* Hewson, Paul
boredom, 103
Breese, Dave, 37-43
Buddhism, 56, 58, 84
Burgess, Andrew J., 27n
Calvin, John, 129-30
Camus, Albert, 25, 43, 156
Chesterton, G. K., 92n
church, 26-32, 41, 48-52, 56-57, 62, 65, 70, 84,
    108-111, 116-23, 135-38
Clark, Kelly James, 127n
Clement of Alexandria, 32-33
communication, 52-54, 111-14, 117, 125, 133
Cooper, John M., 84n
Corsair event, 29-30
Craufurd, Emma, 128n
created, creation, 50, 70, 78-79, 84-92, 98-99,
    101, 107, 129, 136, 139-42, 145, 147-49, 151-54, 161
Dawkins, Richard, 37, 55
defiance, defiant, 99, 101
depression, 97-98
despair, 72, 76, 80, 91-92, 97-101, 103-7, 136,
    155-58
development. *See* human development
Don Juan. *See* aesthetic and Kierkegaard,
    Søren Aabye, works of, *Either/Or*
double danger. *See* love
duty, 90, 106, 109-10, 116, 124
    and love, 139-41
earnestness, 162-63

emotion, 41, 44, 53, 69, 79, 81, 95, 97, 103-4,
    117-18, 130n, 140, 147, 157
Enlightenment, 61, 86, 90, 126
Epictetus, 157n
equality, 77-78, 143-47
ethical (stage or sphere), 42n, 50, 101, 104-10,
    113-14
Evans, C. Stephen, 26, 38n, 39, 46, 130n, 166
evangelism. *See* witness, witnessing
evil, 80, 95n, 103, 131, 135-36, 150-51, 154
existentialism, 25, 38-39, 43, 86, 89
faith, 22, 25, 32-36, 39, 41, 45-48, 53, 55-81, 86,
    93, 97, 108-32, 135-39, 156-59, 162
    Kierkegaard's, 26-28
    leap of, 43-46
    and love, 147-54
Ferreira, M. Jamie, 39n
Feuerbach, Ludwig, 126-28
finite, finitude, 91, 98-99, 103-5, 107
Foley, Michael P., 33, 91
forgiveness, 27-28, 62, 69, 96, 107, 110, 117-18,
    121-22, 125, 161
Francis of Assisi, Saint, 69
freedom, free will, 39, 87-95, 99, 101-2, 104,
    139, 146, 153
Freud, Sigmund, 37, 49-50, 94, 102, 127-28
Garff, Joakim, 29n
gentleness, gentle, 84, 125, 138, 149
    of Jesus, 57, 75-81
gospel, 21, 27, 32-33, 48, 52, 65, 72-73, 111, 115-17,
    122-26, 132-33, 162-63
grace, 32, 57, 66, 111, 163
    abuse of, 70-75
guilt, 50, 67, 72, 80, 96-97, 107, 156
Gutting, Gary, 100n
Hare, John, 106
Hewson, Paul, 58, 60, 64
Hick, John, 131
Hinduism, 55-56
hope, hopeful, 41, 53, 86, 97, 100, 113, 131,
    137-39, 152, 161
    and love, 154-59
human development, 101-8
human nature, 61, 123. *See also* self
Hume, David, 44, 157
humility, humble, 41, 62, 69, 78, 87, 89, 107,
    110, 121, 125, 127, 132, 152

Scripture Index

Finding the Textbook You Need

The IVP Academic Textbook Selector
is an online tool for instantly finding the IVP books
suitable for over 250 courses across 24 disciplines.

ivpacademic.com